T0323901

Cambridge Elements ≡

Elements in Publishing and Book Culture
edited by
Samantha J. Rayner
University College London
Leah Tether
University of Bristol

WOMEN BOOKSELLERS IN THE TWENTIETH CENTURY

Hidden Behind the Bookshelves

Samantha J. Rayner
University College London

CAMBRIDGE
UNIVERSITY PRESS

CAMBRIDGE
UNIVERSITY PRESS

Shaftesbury Road, Cambridge CB2 8EA, United Kingdom

One Liberty Plaza, 20th Floor, New York, NY 10006, USA

477 Williamstown Road, Port Melbourne, VIC 3207, Australia

314–321, 3rd Floor, Plot 3, Splendor Forum, Jasola District Centre,
New Delhi – 110025, India

103 Penang Road, #05–06/07, Visioncrest Commercial, Singapore 238467

Cambridge University Press is part of Cambridge University Press & Assessment,
a department of the University of Cambridge.

We share the University's mission to contribute to society through the pursuit
of education, learning and research at the highest international levels of excellence.

www.cambridge.org
Information on this title: www.cambridge.org/9781108445382

DOI: 10.1017/9781108658584

First published 2025

A catalogue record for this publication is available from the British Library

ISBN 978-1-108-44538-2 Paperback
ISSN 2514-8524 (online)
ISSN 2514-8516 (print)

Women Booksellers in the Twentieth Century

Hidden Behind the Bookshelves

Elements in Publishing and Book Culture

DOI: 10.1017/9781108658584
First published online: January 2025

Samantha J. Rayner
University College London

Author for correspondence: Samantha J. Rayner, s.rayner@ucl.ac.uk

ABSTRACT: The British women booksellers who built and ran successful businesses before, during, and after the Second World War have largely been forgotten. This Element seeks to reclaim some of these histories from where they lie hidden or obscured in archives, accounts of the book trade of the time, and other sources. Though they were often called 'formidable', this research reveals astonishing impact at local, national, and international levels. Divided into four main sections, the Element first gives a literature review of materials about booksellers, before giving a short context to bookselling, the book trade, and book buyers and readers of the early twentieth century. A third section examines the position of women in society at that time, including how they were viewed as part of the book trade; the final section provides histories of nine women booksellers. This title is also available as Open Access on Cambridge Core.

KEYWORDS: bookselling, booksellers, women, book history, publishing history

ISBNs: 9781108445382 (PB), 9781108658584 (OC)
ISSNs: 2514-8524 (online), 2514-8516 (print)

Contents

Introduction

When I started doing the research for this Element back in 2019, just inside the doors of Waterstones Gower Street, 'Europe's largest new and second-hand bookshop',[1] and hidden behind a bookcase, was a modest brass plaque which commemorated Una Dillon, who founded Dillon's University Bookshop in 1957 (see Figure 1). Yet few people today have heard of Dillon, or her contemporary women booksellers, who worked to create new kinds of bookshops and booksellers for new generations of educated, literate readers. This was the starting point for this research: to find out more about Dillon, and write about her bookselling achievements. In doing so, many more women booksellers began to emerge – too many to include comprehensively here, but whose histories, also hidden, show the professionalism and active part they played in the shaping and practice of bookselling during the mid decades of the twentieth century.

This Element brings forward some of these obscured histories, when so much change was happening in London, the UK, and beyond. Christina Foyle, the 'Red Queen of Charing Cross Road'[2] has attracted the most interest from journalists in the past, in the main because of the high-profile connections she had via her literary lunches, but the achievements of other women booksellers show that they ranged widely, from the establishment of world-renowned academic bookshops by Una Dillon and Gerti Kvergic (Dillon's University Bookshop; The Economist Bookshop), key radical bookshops by Eva Collet Reckitt and Margaret Mynatt (Collet's; Central Books), general bookshops in Chelsea by Elizabeth Weiler (The Chelsea Bookshop) and, outside of London, sustained commitment to and influence on bookseller training and bookshop standards by booksellers such as Irene Babbidge, Elise Santoro and Margot Heginbothom (Ibis Library, Banstead; The Book Club, Crowborough; K. J. Bredon's Bookshop, Brighton). In addition, and perhaps hidden under even more layers of historical silt, are

---

[1] See www.waterstones.com/bookshops/gower-street. Accessed 19 January 2022.

[2] Depicted as such by the graphic novelist Hannah Berry on one of 28 panels commissioned by Foyles in 2014. See https://hannahberry.co.uk/work/foyles/. Accessed 20 May 2024.

Figure 1 Photograph of Una Dillon

women like Hilda Light and Mabel Riley, whose work supporting book-sellers more widely shows the breadth of activity, change and improvement going on during this period.

The research for these histories has been painstaking, involving trips to archives (Reading University's Special Collections, Senate House Library Special Collections, the LSE Archive and Special Collections, the BFI Special Collections, the British Library) and the kind help from others who have been generous in trying to help me fill in the gaps (see Acknowledgements). Work has recently been tremendously helped by the digitisation of *The Bookseller* via the British Newspaper Archives: it is no exaggeration to call this a game-changer in terms of time saved, because before this the only way to see if there were references to anyone or anything in that key publication was to go through each edition, page by page. There is still plenty of work to be done, and one of the aims of this Element is to show that it is possible, although not easy, to recreate these histories.

The next section of this Element will provide a selective literature review of work done on UK bookselling in the twentieth and twenty-first centuries, to help underscore both the need for more research to be done on bookselling histories, and also capture the current breadth of books about bookselling, bookselling research more generally, and the reports from booksellers themselves. I hope that this will prove useful for anyone who wants to start investigating bookselling research, and inspire more to happen: there is not room here to provide anything other than snapshots of a few of the women working in and for bookselling at this time, but the exposure of some will lead to more research on others: several more London booksellers await attention (Felicité Gwynne, from John Sandoe Books, for example) and a more comprehensive look at women booksellers in cities outside of London, like Hilda Austick (Austick's Bookshops, Leeds), Hilary Pattinson (A. B. Ward, Sheffield) and Pat Hudson (Hudson's Bookshops, Birmingham) would give a broader picture of what was happening across the UK. It is also of great regret that there was not space here to look at Elsie Bertram's transformative impact on book distribution (Bertram Books), or include more analysis of the way the Booksellers Association helped catalyse the experience offered by these women to embed it within the wider development of bookselling practice in the UK.

To appreciate the contexts within which these women booksellers were working, the third section of this Element will give some historical background to the opportunities and challenges for women during this period, as well as outline the state of bookselling and the book trade in the UK, and consider the challenges raised by the buried or lost archives around these professions. The fourth section will look at some of the women booksellers in more detail, including a longer case study of Una Dillon, and then the conclusion will briefly analyse the impact and value of their work, and next steps for this research.

1 Literature Review on Twentieth- and Twenty-First-Century UK Bookselling

Bookselling has been a largely overlooked aspect of book culture, particularly as it operated and operates in the twentieth and twenty-first centuries in the UK. Of publishing history, and of book history, we have a significant body of scholarship, but of bookshops and bookselling, there is comparatively little published material. As Rick Rylance has pointed out,

> the role of the bookshop in British literary culture … may have been under-appreciated and certainly under-researched.[3]

Ian Norrie, a bookseller and writer who did much work trying to capture some of the histories of British bookselling in the twentieth century, pointed out that

> One obvious reason for [the lack of books about booksellers] is that publishers often indulge their vanity, expecting to make a financial loss excusable on the grounds that the book can also be seen as good publicity for the imprint. Booksellers, similarly motivated, rarely produce anything more imposing than a stapled brochure.[4]

However, this has been changing: the Book Trade Lives project, which ran between 1997 and 2007 via National Life Stories at the British Library Sound Archive captured oral histories from book trade people, including booksellers, and contains valuable evidence;[5] chapters on bookselling have

---

[3] Rick Rylance, *Literature and the Public Good* (Oxford: Oxford University Press, 2016), p. 133.

[4] Ian Norrie and Gary Ink, 'The Literature of the Book: Retail Bookselling', *Logos* 15.3, 2004, p. 164. https://doi-org.libproxy.ucl.ac.uk/10.2959/logo.2004.15.3.164. Accessed 25 April 2024.

[5] My own visit there was in 2019, but the collection has been inaccessible since October 2023 because of the cyber-attack on the British Library. For this reason, all quotations have been taken from the book of the project, edited by

appeared in major volumes like the *Cambridge History of the Book in Britain*,[6] and *The Oxford Handbook of Publishing*;[7] and studies of booksellers in other countries have appeared, too.[8]

The histories and importance of modernist bookshops, in particular, have been looked at in revealing and insightful detail, showing just how valuable a perspective these histories can add to an understanding of cultural developments; Andrew Thacker's work, for example, highlights the part women booksellers played in the construction of an international public for modernism, focussing on Sylvia Beach (Shakespeare and Company, Paris), Adrienne Monnier (La Maison Des Amis des Livres, Paris), and Frances Steloff (Gotham Book Mart, Manhattan). Thacker points out that

> extensive work has been done that has considered modern periodical culture, small presses and publishers, salons, manifestos, movements and isms, as well as other significant features of the modernist marketplace such as celebrity, patronage, and censorship. However, despite the welter of scholarship upon the complex cultural infrastructure that underpinned Anglo-European and American modernism in particular, one of the most important sites of the everyday transaction of the modernist artefact between artist, writer, publisher, and public has been virtually ignored – that is, the humble bookshop.[9]

Sue Bradley, *The British Book Trade: An Oral History* (London: The British Library, 2008).

[6] Iain Stevenson, 'Distribution and Bookselling', in Andrew Nash, Claire Squires, and Ian R. Willison, eds., *The Cambridge History of the Book in Britain*, *Volume VII* (Cambridge: Cambridge University Press, 2019), pp. 191–230.

[7] Niels Peter Thomas, 'Bookselling', in Angus Phillips and Michael Bhaskar, eds., *The Oxford Handbook of Publishing* (Oxford: Oxford University Press, 2019), pp. 399–410.

[8] For example, Fernande Roy 's *Histoire de la librairie au Québec* (Québec: Leméac, 2000); Patricia Sorel, *Petite histoire de la librairie française* (Paris: La Fabrique, 2021).

[9] Andrew Thacker, '"A True Magic Chamber": The Public Face of the Modernist Bookshop', *Modernist Cultures* 11.3, 2016, p. 434.

Huw Osbourne emphasises that Robert Darnton's depiction of booksellers as 'the forgotten middlemen of literature'[10] does not fully represent their agency, because, he says, 'not only were many of these twentieth-century booksellers *middlewomen*, but none of them could be regarded as mere conduits connecting other, more important, elements of the communications circuit'.[11] In the same edited collection, chapters by Ted Bishop, Barbara A. Brannon and Celia Hilliard highlight American women booksellers Madge Jennison and Mary Mowbray Clarke (Sunwise Turn, New York), Marion Dodd and Mary Byers Smith (Hampshire Bookshop) and Fanny Butcher (Chicago Bookshop) respectively,[12] whilst Katy Masuga explores Sylvia Beach's contribution to modernism via Shakespeare and Company in Paris.[13]

This Element looks at some of England's women booksellers working during overlapping periods with their counterparts in other countries listed above, but widens the discussion beyond a modernist focus, to evaluate the variety of contributions these women made to the book trade, to the spread and accessibility of ideas, and to the changes in what a bookshop could be for a reading consumer. In this respect, it is a counter-balance to Matthew Chambers's Element in this series, *London and the Modernist Bookshop*[14] which is a detailed study of a specific area of London, Parton Street, to foreground 'the role of the book trade on modernist bookshops and literary

---

[10] Robert Darnton, *The Kiss of Lamourette: Reflections in Cultural History* (New York: Norton, 1990), p. 128.

[11] Huw Osborne, 'Introduction: Openings', in H. Osborne, ed., *The Rise of the Modernist Bookshop: Books and the Commerce of Culture in the Twentieth Century* (Farnham: Ashgate Publishing Ltd, 2015), pp. 3–4.

[12] Ted Bishop, 'The Sunwise Turn and the Social Space of the Bookshop'; Barbara A. Brando, '"We Have Come to Stay": The Hampshire Bookshop and the Twentieth-Century "Personal Bookshop"'; and Celia Hilliard, '"Lady Midwest": Fanny Butcher – Books', in *The Rise of the Modernist Bookshop*, pp. 31–65, pp. 15–31, and pp. 89–113.

[13] K. Masuga, 'Sylvia and Company', in *The Rise of the Modernist Bookshop* (Farnham: Ashgate Publishing Ltd, 2015), pp. 181–199.

[14] Matthew Chambers, *London and the Modernist Bookshop* (Cambridge: Cambridge University Press, 2020).

modernism'.[15] Chambers also looks at the way David Archer's bookshop on that street was 'very much rooted in local activism'[16] and, as shall be seen later, at least two women booksellers operating in London were to carry on that focus: Eva Collet Reckitt and Margaret Mynatt.

Studies of radical bookselling during this period are greatly aided by the work of Dave Cope and Ross Bradshaw, via the Radical Bookshops group, who have created valuable resources such as the Radical Bookshops Bibliography, a Radical Bookshops Listing, and a series of newsletters which contain histories of some of these shops.[17] Cope's brief history of Central Books, in particular, gives some more insight into Margaret Mynatt, which will be picked up later in this Element. There has also been helpful work done on more contemporary feminist bookselling, via work done by, for example, Lucy Delap and Eileen Cadman, Gail Chester, and Agnes Pivot.[18]

Simon Frost's case study of Southampton's bookselling enterprises around 1900 contains extremely insightful early chapters which discuss commodity culture and readers,[19] and his work on the various bookshops in the city, although in a period earlier to the one in this Element, nonetheless shows the beginnings of a pattern. For although most of the shops selling books in the centre of Southampton were run by men, Frost adds a note to underline research showed that in outlying areas, women seemed to be the ones running smaller, but effective businesses: 'clearly, the periphery offered better opportunities for women than the male-dominated high street'.[20] Frost also provides a useful summary of literature on bookshops, which, as he says, is 'relatively sparse'.[21] He highlights the six editions of Mumby's *Publishing and*

[15] Ibid., p. 5. [16] Ibid., p. 2.

[17] See www.leftontheshelfbooks.co.uk/research.php. Accessed 9 November 2023.

[18] See, e.g., Lucy Delap, 'Feminist Bookshop, Reading Cultures and the Women's Liberation Movement in Great Britain, c.1974–2000', *History Workshop* 81.1, 2016, pp. 171–196; and Eileen Cadman, Gail Chester, and Agnes Pivot, 'Getting the Ideas out: The Problems of Distribution', in *Rolling Our Own: Women as Printers, Publishers, and Distributors* (London: Minority Press Group, 1981), pp. 88–98.

[19] Simon Frost, *Reading, Wanting, and Broken Economics* (New York: SUNY Press, 2021), chapter 1, pp. 21–35.

[20] Ibid., p. 157. [21] Ibid., pp. 45–46.

Bookselling as the main resource available until now on UK booksellers;[22] each edition updates the contents, the later ones significantly, and there is a progression from an emphasis on the publishing half of the title to the gradual expansion of the sections on retail booksellers and bookselling.[23] I will be using these different editions later on to show how the language describing women booksellers shifted: the volumes are themselves revealing products of each period they were published in, giving some contemporary insight into how these women fitted into (or were taken out of) a written account of the history of their trade.

Outside of academia, there has been a clutch of publications on bookshops in recent years. From Robin Ince's entertaining *Bibliomaniac: An Obsessive's Tour of the Bookshops of Britain* – 'in no other shops have I experienced the same delight and passion in what the sellers are doing as I witnessed in all the bookshops I visited'[24] – to James Patterson's *The Secret Lives of Booksellers and Librarians* – 'today's booksellers and librarians are extraordinarily good at understanding and motivating . . . what they do is crucial for this country, especially right now'[25] – books about bookselling are having a moment. Martin Latham's *The Bookseller's Tale*,[26] which

[22] Ibid., p. 45.

[23] The first iteration was published as *The Romance of Bookselling: A History from the Earliest Times to the Twentieth Century*, by Frank Mumby (London: Chapman & Hall, 1910); then followed the first edition of *Publishing and Bookselling*, by Frank Mumby (London: Jonathan Cape, 1930); a New & Revised Edition then appeared, also by Mumby, in 1949 (London: Jonathan Cape, 1949); a third edition by Mumby in 1954 (London: Jonathan Cape, 1954); a Revised & Enlarged Edition, by Mumby and with additions from Max Kenyon, in 1956 (London: Jonathan Cape, 1956), and then a new revised edition, this time including work by Frank Mumby and updates from Ian Norrie (London: Jonathan Cape, 1974). A final, sixth edition was published, but this time called *Mumby's Publishing and Bookselling in the Twentieth Century*, by Ian Norrie (London: Bell & Hyman, 1982).

[24] Robin Ince, *Bibliomaniac: An Obsessive's Tour of the Bookshops of Britain* (London: Atlantic Books, 2022), p. 289.

[25] James Patterson and Matt Eversmann, *The Secret Lives of Booksellers and Librarians: True Stories of the Magic of Reading* (London: Century, 2024), p. viii.

[26] Martin Latham, *The Bookseller's Tale* (London: Particular Books, 2020).

'haphazardly crams knowledge into every corner'[27] just like the best book-shops do, spans bookshops from the Seine to Venice, from New York to Canterbury, and highlights the parts many booksellers, especially those women behind Latham's first foray into bookselling, Sally Slaney and Lesley McKay of Chelsea's Slaney and McKay bookshop, have played in his own career. He notes that Ruth Hadden, the manager of this bookshop, had herself come from Collet's, which, as will be expanded upon later, had been formed by two more redoubtable women booksellers, Eva Collet Reckitt and Olive Parsons.[28] Latham's far-reaching anecdotes and factual forays into bookish history are a constant reminder of 'the unique cultural vantage point which a bookseller can have'.[29]

These cultural perspectives are also explored by Jeff Deutsch, in *In Praise of Good Bookstores*: 'good bookstores reflect their communities; exceptional bookstores both reflect and create their communities'.[30] Moreover, 'we must recognise and then rectify the considerable devaluing of the work of book-sellers in building spaces that contribute to a more learned, more under-standing, and more fulfilled populace'.[31] Deutsch is the former Director of the Chicago Seminary Co-op Bookstores, a non-profit enterprise with a strong mission to create enticing browsing experiences: 'We recognize that, in addition to purchasing books, most of our customers patronize our bookstores in order to interact with a space dedicated to books' explains the website,[32] or, to put it another way, 'The good bookstore sells books, but its primary product . . . is the browsing experience.'[33] This specialness of place, unique perhaps in the retail context, is also dwelt upon in another Element in

---

[27] Katy Guest, '*The Bookseller's Tale* by Martin Latham Review – a Literary Celebration', *The Guardian*, 19 December 2020, www.theguardian.com/books/2020/dec/19/the-booksellers-tale-by-martin-latham-review-a-literary-celebra tion. Accessed 15 February 2024.

[28] Latham, p. 312–313. [29] Ibid., p. 327.

[30] Jeff Deutsch, *In Praise of Good Bookstores* (Princeton: Princeton University Press, 2022), p. 9.

[31] Ibid., p. 17.

[32] 'The Seminary Co-op: A Not-for-profit Bookstore', www.semcoop.com/semin ary-co-op-not-profit-bookstore. Accessed 21 April 2024.

[33] Deutsch, p. 24.

this series, Kristen Highland's *The Spaces of Bookselling: Stores, Streets, and Pages*, where the 'diversity and fluidity of modes of bookselling' attests to the need to examine more closely the 'complex spatial and cultural geographies of bookselling'.[34] Highland's work looks at destination bookstores, itinerant book wagons, street-side book stalls, and the revelations hidden within a bookshop's catalogue. As a result the value of bookselling research to many different fields is made clear, as the tensions 'between commerce and idealism, between belonging and exclusion, and between regulation and innovation' are uncovered and analysed.[35]

Josh Cook's *The Art of Libromancy* is a passionate, fluent, forceful argument for the power of handselling, and why it should matter how books are made and sold to readers. It is a powerful manifesto from a working bookseller who advocates for a progressive model of bookselling which recognises that

> possibility grows when we are a community instead of a collection of individuals, when we see the relationship between booksellers and readers as collaborative rather than transactional, and when we see providing the opportunity for growth as one of the key services independent booksellers provide to their customers.[36]

Danny Caine, too, another active American bookseller, has written a similarly energetic defence of why bookstores need protecting: in short, because they are 'powerful machines for uplifting, celebrating, discovering, and ultimately selling good books'[37] – and these books are 'beyond those that appear on Walmart's shelves'.[38] His work is directed at the reader, encouraging them to be better literary citizens, and to recognise, as Cook's book also stresses,

---

[34] Kristen Highland, *The Spaces of Bookselling: Stores, Streets, and Pages* (Cambridge: Cambridge University Press, 2023), p. 94.

[35] Ibid., p. 95.

[36] Josh Cook, *The Art of Libromancy* (Windsor: Biblioasis, 2023), p. 68.

[37] Danny Caine, *How to Protect Bookstores and Why: The Present and Future of Bookselling* (Portland, OR: Microcosm, 2023), p. 12.

[38] Ibid., p. 13.

> Nobody is better suited to create and nurture a literary community than a group of talented booksellers. On a broad scale, bookstores across the country and around the world are doing valuable work to help readers discover literature, and to advocate for unique and overlooked books.[39]

Both of these books follow on from Andrew Laties's *Rebel Bookseller*,[40] which 'champions the importance of the role of the independent bookseller in our society as Johnny Appleseed sowers of cultural, political, educational, and ideological diversity, even as they foster the shared emotional connection of healthy community life'.[41] Laties, currently a manager of one of the USA's leading children's bookstores, Bank Street, in New York, constructs his book around ten 'rants' which contain both practical information for the would-be bookseller, as well as more philosophical thoughts on the book trade. The 'rants' help to underscore the urgency in the appeals, and the emotion behind the carefully curated advice in many of the chapters: but this is, above all, a provocation:

> This edition calls out beyond prospective booksellers to all indie business owners, as well as to community groups, real estate developers, nonprofit organisations, universities, and urban planners. A revival of locally controlled indie bookselling is essential for fostering the creative, locally autonomous citizenry this nation requires. We all have a role. Now is the time for action.[42]

[39] Ibid., p. 207.

[40] Andrew Laties, *Rebel Bookseller: Why Indie Businesses Represent Everything You Want to Fight For – From Free Speech to Buying Local to Building Communities*, rev. and updated ed. (New York: Seven Stories Press, 2011).

[41] Edward Morrow, 'Foreword: Rebel Booksellers' in *Rebel Bookseller* (New York: Seven Stories Press, 2011), p. 19.

[42] Laties, p. 34.

A decade or so after the new edition was published, American independent booksellers are continuing to push this vision. The Reimagining Bookstores group has been encouraging indies to come together with this appeal:

> We invite you to dream and collaborate together – to reimagine and transform America's bookstores into next-generation community bookstores, to help literary entrepreneurs open new bookstores in book deserts, and to help bookstores strengthen their place in the hearts of their communities as thriving centers for ideas and conversations.[43]

The Bookselling Research Network, which began in 2020, creates a space for all those interested in bookselling-related research to meet, and has members in many countries around the world, allowing for a greater knowledge base of bookselling in different territories.[44] In Europe, the EU-funded RISE (Resilience, Innovation and Sustainability for the Enhancement of Bookselling) body,[45] and in the UK, the Booksellers Association, have both been producing reports on the value of bookshops and the challenges they face,[46] so together all this evidences a period of renewed optimism and action around the bookseller and their place in society: a period I am hoping this

---

[43] Reimagining Bookstores, https://reimaginingbookstores.org/. Accessed 21 April 2024.

[44] The Bookselling Research Network: https://booksellingresearchnet.uk/. Accessed 21 April 2024.

[45] RISE: https://risebookselling.eu/. Accessed 21 April 2024.

[46] Fanny Valembois and David Piovesan, *Study on the Sustainability of the Bookselling Sector: State of Play, Challenges, and Sector Improvements* (RISE Bookselling, 2024); https://risebookselling.eu/wp-content/uploads/2024/03/RISE_Sustainability-report_FULL_EN.pdf Accessed 21st April 2024; Chris Gregory, Dr Regine Sonderland Saga and Professor Cathy Parker, *Booksellers as Placemakers: The Contribution of Booksellers to the Vitality and Viability of High Streets* (Booksellers Association, 2022); www.booksellers.org.uk/BookSellers/media/Booksellers/Booksellers-as-Placemakers-for-website_1.pdf. Accessed 21st April 2024.

Element will show is a continuation of an earlier time with similarly energetic advocates and practitioners.

More pertinently, as this review of literature approaches its end, two very recent publications put forward new histories of women in the book trade: Jane Cholmeley's history of the Silver Moon Bookshop, *A Bookshop of One's Own*, shows, as the sub-heading claims, 'how a group of women set out to change the world' through the setting up of a feminist and lesbian bookshop in the 1980s.[47] In *The Edinburgh Companion to Women in Publishing, 1900–2020*, the editors collect together over thirty chapters on different ways women have changed the book trade world, underlining that there has been little attention 'to the stories of more obscure authors and industry actors, from typesetters to readers, book designers to font makers, secretaries to office managers, booksellers to travellers, illustrators to editors'.[48]

There is one chapter on women booksellers in this volume: not a criticism of a work which tries to cover so much, over so international a scope – but an observation, perhaps, that bookselling is still one of the more Cinderella professions of the book trade world, where work is carried out largely unrecorded and unrecognised, an example of the observation that 'true professionalism often equates to invisibility . . . [which] creates a particularly complex set of considerations for historians engaged in recovery work'.[49] The chapter on women booksellers focuses on bookshops created, as the title of the piece highlights, as 'a room of one's own on the high street': that is, '"personal" bookshops or bookshop salons'.[50] This Element deals with women booksellers

[47] Jane Cholmeley, *A Bookshop of One's Own: How a Group of Women Set Out to Change the World* (London: Mudlark, 2024).

[48] Claire Battershill, Alice Staveley, and Nicola Wilson, 'Making Fields: Women in Publishing', in Nicola Wilson, Claire Battershill, Sophie Heywood et al., eds., *The Edinburgh Companion to Women in Publishing, 1900–2020* (Edinburgh: Edinburgh University Press, 2024), p. 7.

[49] Ibid., p. 8.

[50] Matthew Chambers, 'A Room of One's Own on the High Street: Women Booksellers in Early Twentieth-Century Britain and the United States', in Nicola Wilson, Claire Battershill, Sophie Heywood et al., eds., *The Edinburgh Companion to Women in Publishing* (Edinburgh: Edinburgh University Press, 2024), p. 557.

who, in the main, have been even less visible in history than these sisters whose shops were emphatically 'communal spaces': theirs are less 'intimate affairs',[51] more general bookselling spaces, with women who took an active part in the way bookselling was organised and practiced during the mid twentieth-century period. As Chambers rightly emphasises at the end of his chapter, 'women entering senior positions in bookselling in numbers … was not only a demographic shift but also a shift in the way business was done'.[52]

No introductory section on literature about bookselling would be complete without highlighting the work of Laura J. Miller, whose *Reluctant Capitalists* opened up the research landscape this Element, and all the other texts mentioned above, sits within: she showed how bookshops are the 'site of conflicting visions of how both individual and collective life benefit from the circulation of material goods',[53] and although her focus is on US bookselling, much is of relevance beyond that. She notes that

> People who choose to run an independent bookstore are generally deeply committed to their enterprises; except in the rarest of cases, there is little money to be made, and long hours and tremendous uncertainties are the norm. Independent booksellers consistently describe their work as more than just a way to make a living, and more than just a means of escaping the constraints that come from working for someone else. These booksellers see themselves as bettering society by making books available.[54]

For the women booksellers under examination in this Element, there were additional and varied drivers which enabled them to create successful and unique bookshops, bringing different kinds of bookish culture to readers.

---

[51] Ibid. [52] Ibid., p. 566.

[53] Laura J. Miller, *Reluctant Capitalists: Bookselling and the Culture of Consumption* (Chicago: University of Chicago Press, 2006), p. 6.

[54] Ibid., p. 14.

2 Histories and Contexts

As a specialist kind of retailing, then, bookselling has its own complex set of histories. For several centuries, the term 'bookseller' covered many different roles, including publisher, and often production manager, too. When manuscripts were being written, or early printed books produced, the different parts of the process were often organised by the same person, so that a customer could request what was in effect a bespoke book, every time. The text would be produced by one person, the scribe or printer, then illustrated (if the reader wanted that) by the limner, and then bound in the binding of choice by the binder. The bookseller oversaw all these processes for the customer, and drew profit from the combined exertions of the various skilled workers who pulled the required book together. As time went on, some of these roles were absorbed into the printing part of the process, so that production was managed by one organisation, but right up until the nineteenth century the role of publisher was often still that of bookseller as well. Well-known publishing names like Macmillan, and Longmans, which still survive today, are examples of this.[55]

By the start of the twentieth century, however, bookshops were independent entities, with booksellers organising themselves to form the Associated Booksellers of Great Britain and Ireland (AB),[56] a body that oversaw the putting together of the Net Book Agreement (NBA), which fixed prices for books so that no matter where a customer bought a copy from, the price would be the same. This Agreement, which was also approved by the Society of Authors and the Publishers Association, came into effect in 1900, and had a profound impact on the way books were sold in the UK. It is no exaggeration to say that before this, many bookshops were struggling to keep going because of the lack of fixed prices for books: indeed, as the account of the first fifty years of the AB underlines, when the

---

[55] For some more information about this, see 'Fathers and Sons' chapter in Ian Norrie, *Mumby's Publishing and Bookselling in the Twentieth Century* (London: Bell & Hyman, 1982), pp. 28–40.

[56] The name was changed to Booksellers Association in 1948; both terms are used in this Element, reflecting relevant time periods.

first meeting of the Association happened on 23 January 1895, at Stationers' Hall in London, the booksellers met

> to remedy immediate and desperate ills. Their object was to prevent the complete collapse of retail bookselling, and the remedy they had joined together to support was the principle of a net price for books.[57]

The key booksellers involved in this endeavour were men: Henry W. Keay, F. Calder Turner, Edwin Pearce, Thomas Burleigh, and F. A. Denny, as well as Robert Maclehose, Robert Bowes, Benjamin H. Blackwell, and F. Hanson. The early years of the twentieth century saw booksellers working with publishers to implement the NBA, and then fighting the so-called Book War, when *The Times* newspaper started a book subscription service which tried to get around the NBA's rules. No sooner had all this died down than the First World War started, and booksellers such as Basil Blackwell and George Brimley Bowes (sons of those mentioned above) became 'new men to meet the new age'.[58]

Many of the names of the London bookshops of this early twentieth-century period have now been lost: Truslove & Hanson, J. & E. Bumpus, Wyman & Son, Alfred Wilson, A. R. Mowbray, Barker & Howard.[59] Hatchard's and Foyle's are still familiar, however, and, as shall be seen, many new names were to spring up during the twenties and thirties.[60]

---

[57] William G. Corp, *Fifty Years: A Brief Account of the Associated Booksellers of Great Britain and Ireland 1895–1945* (Oxford: Basil Blackwell, 1948), p. 5.

[58] Ibid., p. 33.

[59] See Frank A. Mumby and Ian Norrie, *Publishing and Bookselling*, 5th Ed. (London: Jonathan Cape, 1974), pp. 368–379.

[60] Mumby and Norrie, 5th Ed., p. 378. According to Norrie, Ward's was the first modern bookshop in London: 'Ward set out to challenge the image of the traditional bookshop, with its window displays built up so as to obscure the inside of the shop from the street . . . and its sanctified air of an old, dusty, ill-lit library. His shop had light oak shelves, fittings by Heal's, and fitted carpet, and its window was low and open, attracting the customers in to the books which they could see so alluringly arranged in the interior.'

Bookselling in Britain after the end of the First World War was still an extremely serious, male-dominated business, as the details above shows. Booksellers saw their role as cultural, moral, and even spiritual caretakers to the reading public, evidenced by frequent impassioned speeches recorded in the industry journals of the period. In a 1924 paper about bookselling by writer and publisher Michael Sadleir, called 'Servants of Books', he claimed:

> The essence of this job, of course, and it is the best job in the world, is loyal service to the book itself. The books demand from their servants not only enthusiasm, not only loyalty, but also practical good sense. No country is the happier for being governed without economic reason, and we are governing one of the most important spiritual countries within the British Empire – the country of the mind. If we govern with obstinate wrong-headedness, with personal jealousies, or with foolish prodigality, we fail in our duty to the public and also insult the majesty and lower the dignity of the sovereign book.[61]

Although this sounds awkwardly jingoistic, during that interwar period there was a determination to create a world where another war on the scale of 1914–1918 would never happen again. Literature was seen as an effective tool in that effort: so it was also the period in which reading material proliferated:

> Factors which should have deflated the market – paper rationing, almost prohibitive production costs, mass unemployment, and the expansion of the cinema and wireless – seem to have had the opposite effect: they unexpectedly promoted the reading habit and thereby preserved demand. This continued demand for all classes for light fiction, coupled with the necessity to restore revenues drained during the First World War, accelerated the process of

[61] Michael Sadleir, 'Servants of Books: Their Privileges and Duties', *The Bookseller and the Stationery Trades Journal* (October 1924), p. 80; and *The Publishers' Circular and Booksellers' Record* (4 October 1924), p. 469.

commercialization initiated by the Victorians and allowed
a more intense exploitation of the market.[62]

This growth, especially for lighter fiction, was accompanied by the continued presence of the subscription library; by 1928 a report to the Society of Bookmen could claim that between a quarter and two-thirds of all books published went to the big four circulating libraries (Mudie's, W. H. Smith, *The Times* Book Club, and Boots). For some idea of scale, in 1920 Boots had around 200 libraries in Britain attached to their pharmacies, and by 1938 there were 460 branches.[63]

In 1921, the Newbolt Report was published, which looked at the teaching of English across all age ranges. Included in it is this passage on the key part bookshops and booksellers play:

> An educated bookseller is in a position to render great service to the community; and we believe that the English teachers of the near future will, in turn, be glad to lend such a benefactor all the assistance in their power to encourage their pupils to become his customers. In every town the bookselling shop should become, what in University cities and in one or two other favoured spots, it is already, a centre of literary and artistic interests and enlightenment; a place where the best books, old and new, can be inspected at leisure.[64]

As educational access began to expand, and as publishing began to adapt to all these new contexts, bookshops saw themselves as crucial quality control agents. Major G. Brimley Bowes, the great nephew of Daniel and Alexander

---

[62] Joseph McAleer, *Popular Reading and Publishing in Britain 1914–1950* (Oxford: Clarendon Press, 1992), p. 42.

[63] See Nicola Wilson, 'Boots Book-lovers' Library and the Novel: The Impact of a Circulating Library Market on Twentieth Century Fiction', *Information and Culture*, 49.4, 2014, p. 429.

[64] *The Newbolt Report*, 1921, p. 330. See www.educationengland.org.uk/documents/newbolt/newbolt1921.html. Accessed 19 January 2022.

Macmillan, had set up a bookshop in Cambridge, and was a frequent com-
mentator on bookselling during this period. He pushed the Bookseller's
Association to establish more formalised training programmes, saying:

> If a licence is required to mark those qualified to dispense
> medicine for those who are or may be sick, and to prevent
> the misapplication of what may poison their bodies, why not
> a licence to mark those who are qualified to dispense healthy
> and good literature for all readers, and prevent the dissemi-
> nation of books which might poison their minds?[65]

This view of the bookseller as crucial arbiter of taste aligned with arguments
vigorously discussed in the press in the 1920s, by men such as the journalist
Sidney Dark and the publisher Stanley Unwin. In 1922 a published account of
Dark's lecture to the Society of Bookmen appeared. In this he underlined the
responsibility that all those working in the book trade had towards a 'New
Reading Public', 'that ever-increasing company drawn from what we com-
monly call the lower middle class and the working class',[66] stressing that

> The wider you make the area of appreciation of the mas-
> terpieces of literature, the more general genuine culture
> becomes, the more probable it must be that social abuses
> will almost automatically disappear, because abuses are the
> result of narrowness of vision and selfish stupidity, and
> when men walk in the light they avoid the pitfalls and
> stand in little peril of falling into the abyss.[67]

He noted the popularity of literature which people read simply to forget,
denouncing them as 'narcotics' which are 'as destructive of real life and

---

[65] Major G. Brimley Bowes, 'Education and the Book Trade', *The Bookseller and Stationery Trades Journal*, August 1920, p. 530.

[66] Sidney Dark, *The New Reading Public: A Lecture Delivered under the Auspices of the Society of Bookmen* (London: Allen & Unwin, 1922), pp. 5–6.

[67] Ibid., p. 10.

living as cocaine'.[68] Philip Unwin also used this phrase, 'New Reading Public', in an influential article he wrote for *The Bookseller* in 1934, where he drew comparisons between newspaper and book readers, and berated the book trade for not yet securing the support of this new readership in the same way as the newspaper proprietors had managed to do. He, like Faber had done a few years earlier (see below) laid the fault firmly at the feet of booksellers, who had not made their shops appealing enough, and who had not tried to attract these new readers.[69] His article had so much impact that it became the focus of a weekend conference at Ripon Hall, Oxford, in September 1934, when over 50 booksellers and publishers gathered to discuss this new readership, and how to respond to them.[70]

In an article in *The Nation and Athenaeum* as part of a series looking at Books and the Public,[71] bookseller Charles Young asserts that

> The selling of books affects the intellectual life of the people very nearly, combining with the Artist and Teacher and in fact becoming their introducer to the public in furthering new ideas and explaining old ones; there is no better way. Booksellers therefore should cultivate a good literary judgement for the benefit of the public and not regard their calling merely as a commercial venture.[72]

In 1931, Geoffrey Faber, talking to the AB, praised the establishment, in 1925, of a National Book Council to promote books and encourage reading for leisure, but warned booksellers not to rely on that organisation to bring book-buyers to them. He calls it a matter 'of national importance' that

---

[68] Ibid., p. 12.

[69] Philip Unwin, 'The New Reading Public', *The Bookseller*, 5 April 1934, p. 184.

[70] It's worth noting that Allen Lane was an attendee at this conference – a timely event given that Penguins were to launch in the following year.

[71] These articles were collected and republished by the Hogarth Press in 1927 under this title.

[72] Charles Young, 'Books and the Public: The Bookseller's Point of View', *The Nation and Athenaeum*, 16 April 1927, pp. 43–44.

readership should be increased in a time when political, economic, moral and religious challenges were 'pressing upon us for solution'. It follows, then, in Faber's words, that 'bookselling ... is an affair of national importance', too: 'bookselling is a national function as well as a business'.[73]

In claiming this importance for booksellers on the national mind and character, these articles connect to key work by literary critics of the time who were also exercised by this new kind of reader: Virginia Woolf famously re-uses Samuel Johnson's term of 'common reader' to describe someone who

> differs from the critic and the scholar. He is worse educated, and nature has not gifted him so generously. He reads for his own pleasure rather than to impart knowledge ... he never ceases, as he reads, to run up some rickety and ramshackle fabric which shall give him temporary satisfaction of looking sufficiently like the real object to allow of affection, laughter, and argument. Hasty, inaccurate, and superficial ...[74]

Q. D. Leavis, writing about *Fiction and the Reading Public* in 1932, sets out the wide variety of reading materials available to the reader (via libraries, newsagents, chemists, book clubs, branches of Woolworth's – and, of course, bookshops)[75] and details how the common reader 'has now not even a glimpse of the living interests of modern literature, is ignorant of its growth and so prevented from developing with it, and that the critical minority to whose sole charge modern literature has now fallen is isolated, disowned by the general public and threatened with extinction'.[76]

The 1930s saw the arrival of the Book Society book club in Britain, the start of Book Tokens, the growth of the Twopenny Libraries, with branches

---

[73] Talk given on 20 May 1931, and included in Geoffrey Faber, *A Publisher Speaking* (London: Faber, 1934), pp.70–71.

[74] Virginia Woolf, *The Common Reader, Vol. I*, ed. Andrew MacNeillie (London: Vintage, 2003), p. 1. (First published by The Hogarth Press in 1925.)

[75] References are taken from Queenie D. Leavis, *Fiction and the Reading Public* (London: Pimlico, 2000). The book was first published by Chatto & Windus in 1932.

[76] Leavis, p. 35.

everywhere, and, of course, the rise of the paperback via the growing success of Penguin books. These years were not easy ones for the bookseller. The increase in books being published had risen from around 7,000 in 1918 to some 14,600 in 1937, so that 'for the harassed bookseller it had become an insoluble problem to pick and choose the worth-while books among the unending stream'.[77]

During this interwar period, this rise in the number of publications[78] and rise in demand for reading material helped begin to shift approaches to what a bookshop should stock. Allen Lane captured the zeitgeist best when, in an article for *The Bookseller* explaining his rationale for the Penguin paperbacks, he said:

> The great majority of the public, which must include many potential bookbuyers, are scared of walking through our doors [i.e., those of bookshops] ... They feel at home in a tuppeny library or at Woolworths, where they get the same amount of attention if they spend 5s or if they go out with nothing at all; but the idea of braving an empty bookshop with two or three assistants lying in wait behind the shelves is too much for them.[79]

The public could buy books from a variety of outlets now, and Lane, who had initially failed to get any bookshop to take on his paperbacks, found success by selling them via Woolworth's. Bookshops did not take long to rethink their approach to the Penguins, and other paperback brands, and as the debate about suitable reading material raged in the popular press, and in book trade periodicals, new shops opened, specialist, general, and academic, which targeted different communities in different ways: Collet's Bookshop, for example, which opened in 1934, on London's Charing Cross Road,

---

[77] Frank Mumby, *Publishing and Bookselling: A History from the Earliest Times to the Present Day* (London: Jonathan Cape, 1949), p. 343.

[78] Books published rose from about 7,000 in 1918 to around 14,600 in 1933, and then 17,000 in 1938. (See ibid., p. 344.)

[79] Allen Lane, 'All about the Penguin Books', *The Bookseller*, 22 May 1935, p. 497.

specialised in left-wing books (see section on Eva Collet Reckitt for more information). It was also the site that Allen Lane chose to locate the first Penguin books vending machine, the Penguincubator, in 1937, and the first company to open a specific Penguin bookshop in 1962.

Booksellers bemoaned the popularity of the 'sixpennies', claiming that they stole profit and distracted customers: before the advent of Penguin the complaint had been that people did not buy enough books. The middle class, said Peter Ibbetson in 1927 'are sponging on writers and publishers, and making it impossible to supply at a reasonable price and a fair profit the commodity they consume ... they read books, but they do not buy them',[80] and the esteemed economist John Maynard Keynes weighed in on this issue, too, laying out the arithmetic of book production and concluding:

> Is it not a thing to be ashamed of, having regard to the wealth and population of the English-speaking world, that editions are on so miserable a scale? How many people spend even £10 a year on books? How many spend 1 per cent of their incomes? To buy a book ought to be felt not as an extravagance, but as a good deed, a social duty which blesses him who does it.[81]

In the later 1930s, booksellers were struggling with the rapid changes of demand from a book-hungry consumer who could now afford to buy a book or two a week. This was great for the reader, but less of a positive for the bookseller. Stanley Unwin explained:

[80] Peter Ibbetson, 'On the Reluctance to Buy Books', *The Nation and Athenaeum*, 5 March 1927, p. 753.

[81] John M. Keynes, 'Are Books Too Dear?', *The Nation and Athenaeum*, 12 March 1927, p. 788. He goes on, 'I should like to mobilise a mighty army, outnumbering Frothblowers and Gugnuncs and Mustard Clubmen, an army of bookworms, pledged to spend £10 a year on books, and in the higher ranks of the Brotherhood, to buy a book a week.' Looking up what these three intriguingly named groups were has been a wonderful side-hustle of this research!

> If it could be proved – and it is much less certain than is
> usually supposed – that sixpenny reprints created or fostered
> a new reading public, the case for them would be over-
> whelming, but if the evidence shows that their effect is
> primarily a transference of demand by regular book-
> buyers from 2s 6d and 3s 6d cloth bound reprints, there is
> not the same cause for rejoicing.[82]

However, Unwin's scepticism around new readers was challenged a week
after his piece appeared in the press, by Margaret Cole (an active socialist
politician, writer, and poet). She argued that there could be no doubt that

> the modern publishers of cheap editions, from Readers'
> Union and the Left Book Club to Penguin Books, have
> found and fostered a new *book-buying* public ... There is
> direct evidence, in the letters of school children, adolescents,
> and pensioners living on tiny incomes; there is also the
> unquestionable evidence of sales.[83]

Her article goes on to outline the issues around book snobbery in the UK,
calling this 'a peculiarly English phenomenon' and a real problem. A liberal
education, so much a preserve for the upper classes, and a way to access wide
reading, has been out of the reach of the ninety per cent of children in the
country who have only had access to an elementary education, and who,
therefore, feel 'a definite inferiority in entering a bookshop'.[84] She challenges
Unwin's concern about consumers avoiding the higher priced books, saying
that she finds it far more likely that 'a taste for reading induced by buying
a new Penguin will lead to a discriminative appreciation of and desire to
possess, and to save up for, such a book as "Mathematics for the Million" or

---

[82] Stanley Unwin, 'Concerning Sixpennies', *The Times Literary Supplement*,
19 November 1938, p. 737.

[83] Margaret Cole, 'Books for the People', *The Times Literary Supplement*,
26 November 1938, p. 751.

[84] Ibid.

a Nonesuch Press edition'.[85] Her views had been honed in a series of articles written a year earlier, for *The Listener*,[86] under the title of 'Books for the Multitude', and would be further worked on to appear as one of the Hogarth Press's Day by Day pamphlets, *Books and the People*.[87] These outputs give a considered and detailed assessment of the different ways people were borrowing and buying reading material at this point, advocating for a democratisation of books via careful quality control of production of the new lines, and a willingness to look at adapting and evolving ways of getting books to readers, rather than rejecting these 'blindly'.[88]

Cole's spotlight on *where* people were buying or borrowing books was a valuable precursor to the work of the Mass Observation project in this area. In a 1942 report on 'Books and the Public', the lack of bookshops in country districts and the working class parts of cities 'accentuates the position where poorer people are less book-buying minded', demonstrating that the distribution of bookshops 'is partly conditioned by traditional factors belonging to a time when there was a much lower standard of general education'.[89] It would be misleading, therefore, the report goes on, to assume that these people are less capable of absorbing and becoming interested in books:

> much less has been done to draw them into the net of book readership than for better off people . . . to a more considerable extent than has apparently been recognised, the bringing of

[85] Ibid.

[86] Margaret Cole, 'Books for the Multitude I: Reading Without Buying', *The Listener*, 22 December 1937, pp. 1388–1389; 'Books for the Multitude II', *The Listener*, 29 December 1937, pp. 1436–1437; 'Books for the Multitude III', *The Listener*, 5 January 1938, pp. 42–43; 'Books for the Multitude IV', *The Listener*, 12 January 1938, pp. 95–96.

[87] Margaret Cole, *Books and the People* (London: Hogarth Press, 1938).

[88] Cole, 'Books for the Multitude IV', p. 96.

[89] Section XVII, 'Channels of Book Buying', p. 41, from Books and the Public. [File Report]. At: Place: University of Sussex. Available through: Adam Matthew, Marlborough, Mass Observation Online, www.massobservation .amdigital.co.uk.libproxy.ucl.ac.uk/Documents/Details/FileReport-1332. Accessed 3 August 2023.

> book interest to the poorest people is therefore largely a matter
> of chance, and in the ordinary pattern of their shopping and
> shop window gazing, they could pass a whole year without
> ever seeing a book on sale.[90]

There was, of course, a significant shift in retail during the interwar period, not just within bookselling, but across all of the major shop types.[91] A growing demand for different goods, from a public eager to embrace the modern, and initially economically buoyant, age, brought with it an influx of new shop designs following the 1925 Paris Exhibition, with a move towards cleaner, and less fussy lines, and a push to create stronger brand identities for chains like Marks & Spencer and Boots. These stores helped encourage shoppers into spaces they had not had access to before, and began to build a flourishing new kind of high street in towns across England. Woolworth, for instance, opened their first store in Liverpool in 1909, but by 1939 had 760 branches.[92] Their shops adopted a 'version of modern architecture still frowned upon by purists', with less of a historicist approach, but, as Kathryn Morrison goes on to point out, this was because they were using architectural design 'to lure – or more likely to avoid intimidating – their target clientele', who were working-class.[93] Later, this Element will explore how Una Dillon used shop design to help create a new bookshop to attract a wide customer base, using interior creativity to complement the architecturally ornate exteriors of the premises she took over.

With the rise of the department and chain stores came more opportunities for bookselling: Thomas Joy, who managed both the library and the book departments in Harrods between 1933 and 1945, said the store was regarded by many 'as the "university" of the department store world'

---

[90] Ibid., p. 42.

[91] See Lawrence E. Neal, *Retailing and the Public* (London: Allen & Unwin, 1932) for a full discussion of the various kinds of shops of the period.

[92] Kathryn Morrison, 'Woolworth: adding character to the British high street, 1909–1939', *History of Retailing and Consumption* 2:2, 2016, p. 89, https://doi .org/libproxy.ucl.ac.uk/10.1080/2373518X.2016.1208945.

[93] Ibid., p. 87.

reflecting that he thought his time there was the making of him, changing him 'from bookman to a business man with a specialised knowledge of the book trade'.[94] Joy went on to manage the Army and Navy Stores at Westminster, and then became managing director of Hatchard's in Piccadilly; he was 'an integral part of the essentially friendly book trade of his time',[95] becoming President of the Booksellers Association in 1957, and 'served on innumerable trade committees and charities, helped count-less authors with their problems, initiated better conditions for staff and devised original methods of salesmanship'.[96] Despite his many achieve-ments, which helped increased awareness of the bookselling world as a business, and despite the fact that he called himself a feminist, declaring that 'women are much stronger than is generally imagined and just as well equipped mentally' for bookselling,[97] his autobiography rarely gives credit to any of the 'thousands' he claimed to have managed,[98] but there is one intriguing mention of a Miss Riley, his secretary at Harrod's 'who was also fully qualified in both bookselling and commercial librarianship' and who helped Joy build 'a first-class and flourishing library service with an ever-increasing membership'.[99] Further research reveals Mabel Riley is thanked for typing all Joy's books, for undertaking research, and compil-ing indexes,[100] and has a dedication in *The Truth about Bookselling*: 'to Miss Mabel Riley, Librarian, Army & Navy Stores Ltd., Personal Member and Member of the Education Board of the Booksellers Association, who for many years has been diligent in organizing classes in London, and without whose persistence and help it is unlikely that this book would ever

[94] Thomas Joy, *Mostly Joy: A Bookman's Story* (London: Michael Joseph, 1971), p. 94.

[95] Ian Norrie, 'Thomas Joy', *The Independent*, 2 May 2003, p. 22.

[96] 'Thomas Joy; Doyen of the book trade who ran the library at Harrods before becoming the head of Hatchards in Piccadilly', *Daily Telegraph* [London], 23 April 2003. *Gale OneFile: News*, link.gale.com/apps/doc/A100478691/STND?u=ucl_ttda&sid=bookmark-STND&xid=307eb121. Accessed 3 August 2023.

[97] Joy, p. 93.   [98] Ibid.   [99] Ibid., p. 153.

[100] See Thomas Joy, 'Acknowledgements', in *The Bookselling Business* (London: Pitman, 1974), pp. vi–vii.

have been completed'.[101] Clearly Miss Riley was so much more than a 'secretary': Joy wrote her obituary in *The Bookseller*, noting that she 'served the Booksellers Association in many ways but is particularly remembered for her painstaking work on the Education Committee'.[102] Indeed, far from just supporting Joy's own bookselling career, Miss Riley is credited with having had 'an exceptionally long and distinguished career in bookselling': she started at Truslove and Hanson, aged 16, in 1919, and then, after moving to a post as Joy's secretary at Harrod's Library in 1936, was given charge of the trade section. She then moved to the Army & Navy Stores where she was Head Librarian. Like the other women booksellers highlighted in section four, Miss Riley gave much time to the professionalisation of her trade: in her case focussing on the training of bookshop assistants. She arranged and supervised courses in London for 20 years, and was the first woman chairman of the London Branch, Booksellers Association Associates.[103]

Another key woman who worked for booksellers was Hilda Light, who was Secretary to the Booksellers Association between 1929 and 1946: 'in Miss H. M. Light the Council found a Secretary whose capabilities and devotion to the Association's interests were to prove of inestimable value'.[104] Her history was one of the most rewarding to uncover, for not only was she credited as being 'a very great lady of the book trade',[105] helping to transform the Association and to build collaborations between the booksellers and the publishers, but she was also a hockey player of some renown, captaining the British women's team in 1924, and going on to be president of both the All England Womens Hockey Association (1931–1945) and the International Federation of Womens Hockey Associations (1951–1953). Her obituary in *The Times* emphasised that

> As an administrator and rules maker she was in a class apart
> and had that clarity of mind that made even those who could

[101] Thomas Joy, *The Truth about Bookselling* (London: Sir Isaac Pitman, 1964), p. v.

[102] Thomas Joy, 'Mabel Constance Riley', *The Bookseller*, 22 January 1993, p. 9.

[103] 'Farewell Party at Hatchards', *The Bookseller*, 8 November 1975, pp. 2320–2321.

[104] Corp, p. 48.

[105] Frank D. Sanders, 'Miss H. M. Light', *The Bookseller*, 8 November 1969, p. 2486.

not go all the way with her ideas listen and consider with the
utmost respect.[106]

When she stepped down from the role of Secretary, the President of the AB,
Mr F. J. Aldwinckle, praised her contribution: 'her meticulous attention to
detail and wide experience of Association matters have been an invaluable
help to the officers and members of council'.[107] Her impact was such that
this was followed by a separate article in *The Bookseller* later that year,
which gives more insight into her achievements:

> no-one could have worked harder to uphold the rights of the
> bookseller than she did . . . she always seemed . . . to be at her
> very best when organising the annual conferences of the
> Association. It was a big responsibility for a woman, but
> never on any occasion [was she] flustered or out of temper.[108]

The article goes on to outline Light's outstanding work during the War,
when at the height of the bombing in London, 'not once did she fail to arrive
at the office – very often after a hazardous journey of detours, and very
often miles of walking'. When Paternoster Row was destroyed, including
the offices of the AB, and all the records disappeared, 'she started off right
away and went to it with a grim determination to get it all together again
with the least possible delay'.[109] The fondness the trade felt for her is shown
in a snippet recording the reaction when a year after her retirement, she
went to the annual conference of the AB in Blackpool: 'Miss Light was
given a rapturous welcome.'[110] She continued to work for the International
Federation of Womens Hockey Associations after her retirement, and was
clearly comfortable and effective using her talents in an international
context: 'she had a sincere feeling for a truly world-wide body of people,

---

[106] 'Miss Hilda Light: International Hockey Player', *The Times*, 3 October 1969, p. 12.

[107] 'Miss Light Retiring', *The Bookseller*, 20 June 1946, p. 813.

[108] Elizabeth Edmonds, 'Miss Light of the A.B.G.B.I.', *The Bookseller*, 17 October 1946, p. 668.

[109] Ibid. [110] 'An Historic Conference', *The Bookseller*, 14 June 1947, p. 887.

drawn together in amity through their common interest in hockey'.[111] Hilda Light operated as a key person in both bookselling and hockey, at a very high level; her input helped both associations move forwards significantly. For the book trade, 'the Publishers Association as well as the Booksellers Association owe much to that charming but formidable lady that was Miss Hilda M. Light'.[112] Despite this, Norrie reduces her accomplishments into this rather underwhelming summary:

> Hilda Light regarded it as her duty to harry the enemy, which is how she saw publishers, according to her opposite number at the PA, Frank Sanders, who found her 'charming burt formidable'. She captained England at hockey and brought the tough qualities demanded on the sports field into the secretarial and conference room.[113]

This is a good point to move on to examine more women booksellers of the twentieth century, who disprove Joy's conviction that 'women are not good at the top'.[114] However, it is worth stressing that his autobiography does demonstrate, in excluding any mention of his female counterparts, why these women have remained in the shadows of history for so long. Miss Riley is a paratextual element, despite her obviously key role in Joy's successful book trade career, and in wider bookselling work.

[111] Majorie Pollard, ed., *Hilda M. Light: Her Life and Times* (London: All Womens Hockey Association, 1972), p. 53.

[112] Sanders, 'Miss H. M. Light', p. 2487.

[113] *Publishing and Bookselling*, 6th Ed., p. 24.

[114] *The Truth about Bookselling*, p. 39.

3 Women and Bookselling

In all these contexts mentioned above, where bookselling and the book trade were changing so rapidly, along with the growing chances women had to go to university and continue their education, women could – and did – participate, not just as assistants, but as business owners. Just as the post-First-World-War landscape changed the opportunities for women in other professions, so too did it increase the need for capable booksellers, and in the next forty years or so, women booksellers were to demonstrate how innovative, effective, and committed they could be.

However, this was not an easy or a straightforward trajectory. The War had resulted in the deaths of nearly three-quarters of a million soldiers; women found themselves with more active places in society open to them, through necessity: 'this was the era of the spinster . . . at last, after so many years of being grudged the right to exist at all, she came into her own'.[115] During the War women had found employment in munitions, in farmwork, in administrative roles, in transport, nursing, factory work, teaching: they were needed, and they stepped up. When the men started to come back from the Front, however, women, under the Pre-War Practices Act, had to relinquish a great many of these jobs in favour of the returning male workforce:

> Since the middle of 1915 they had been gallant workers, for
> whom no praise could be too fulsome; admired, with affec-
> tionate amusement for 'playing the man' like Shakespeare's
> Rosalind. But now the masquerade was over; it was time to
> hang up the doublet and hose behind the kitchen door and
> get back to skirt and aprons, to keep an eye on the clock so
> that the breadwinner's hot tea could be slapped down in
> front of him the second he got in.[116]

---

[115] Ruth Adam, *A Woman's Place* (reissue, London: Persephone Books, 2000), p. 138.

[116] Ibid., pp. 96–97.

Even when they kept their jobs, the pay was often much less than their male counterparts; the 1921 census showed that women were back to being in only a very few occupations (33% in domestic service, 12% in the textile industries, 11% in the clothing trade and 4% in teaching).[117] In 1918 and then in 1928, women were granted voting rights, but it is worth remembering this was still a society where many professions banned married women from jobs, like the Civil Service. Women had been able to attend universities since the second half of the nineteenth century, with London colleges awarding degrees from 1878; but Oxford did not allow this until 1920, and Cambridge, 1948. In 1929 Virginia Woolf's *A Room of One's Own* was published, detailing the challenges women faced but also stressing the opportunities now open to them:

> May I also remind you that most of the professions have been open to you for close on ten years now? When you reflect upon these immense privileges and the length of time during which they have been enjoyed, and the fact that there must be at this moment some two thousand women capable of earning five hundred a year in one way or another, you will agree that the excuse of lack of opportunity, training, encouragement, leisure, and money no longer holds good.[118]

The tone of frustration which comes through here obscures the amount of extraordinary achievements by women during the first decades of the twentieth century, however, and Woolf's arguments swing from pointing out how much else women had to do, and how little space and support they had to carry out any kind of intellectual or creative endeavour, to this admonishment at the end. Although there is not space here to outline these in much detail, just focussing on women in book-related roles shows how varied and influential their contributions were: apart from Woolf and the other women

---

[117] Ibid., pp.101–102.

[118] Virginia Woolf, *A Room of One's Own*, originally published in London by the Hogarth Press in 1929; (edition used here: London: Penguin Modern Classics, 2000), p.111.

in the Bloomsbury Group, this period saw writers such as Dorothy L. Sayers and Agatha Christie navigate the new space created by a democratisation of culture to write successful novels for everyone. Women began to take on significant roles in publishing in the 1930s and 1940s, with Eunice Frost's appointment at Penguin in 1936, and Diana Athill's with Allan Wingate in 1945. Frost was the first woman to receive an OBE for services to literature in publishing (in 1961); Athill was given the Order of the British Empire (in 2009). These were women who made a key impact on the bookish landscape in the UK, and who paved the way for many others who followed them, like Kaye Webb (Puffin), and Carmen Calill (Virago).

It was a very complex set of social, political, and economic contexts, therefore, in which the women in this study worked, and built up their bookshop businesses, and their achievements were all the more remarkable because of these.

Within their own time, however, these achievements were largely hidden; in 1951, when most of the booksellers in this Element were active, a manual called *The Practice of Bookselling* was published, written by B. N. Langdon-Davies.[119] He was the manager of the Bookselling Department of the Welwyn Garden City Stores, a position which earns his book this endorsement from Hubert M. Wilson, who owned Alfred Wilson's Bookshop in London: 'it holds out to the reader a high ideal of bookselling which, it is well known, the writer has himself carried into effect with resounding success'.[120] These high ideals included a chapter on the 'Choice of Assistants', which contains some sharp reminders of just what kind of context women in the book trade were working within: Langdon-Davies lays out, as matters of fact, that bookshop managers (the assumption is very clearly that these are male) have to make do with mainly female unskilled and part-time staff, and that this causes challenging issues. The main one, he says, is 'that most women

---

[119] Langdon-Davies had an eclectic career; he was lecturer in internationalism before the 1914 war, manager of the Labour Publishing Company and other publishing houses, a hotel in Corsica, and the publicity department of Cresta Silks Ltd, as well as an Urban District Councillor for Welwyn Garden City.

[120] Hubert M. Wilson, 'Introduction', in Bernard N. Langdon-Davies, ed., *The Practice of Bookselling* (London: Phoenix House Ltd, 1951), p. x.

have other calls and duties, which admittedly transcend in importance their daily work in the world of industry, and most men do not'.[121] The Angel in the house, with her sacred duties as wife and mother, is given respectful acknowledgement, it seems, but Langdon-Davies then goes on to declare that even if a woman does not have a husband or children or parents to call upon their time, 'she requires, owing to impulses deep in her nature, more time off for shopping, for having her hair dressed and half a dozen other things'.[122] Having thus defined the whole of the female sex, Langdon-Davies muses that

> in this there is at all events one consolation. As a result of factors mentioned above, not many women are out for the more responsible and much fewer posts in the business world. They are therefore more content, if they are reasonably happy in their work and reasonably attached to their colleagues and employers, to stay put – at all events until the call to their real vocation comes.[123]

No evidence remains (at least in so far as I have been able to find to date) of what any of the women booksellers felt about such denigrating descriptions, but given that, as this Element will show, women were proving themselves more than capable of succeeding in this male-dominated book trade, such attitudes are indicative of just how challenging prejudices against women could be.[124]

Indeed, things appeared more optimistic in the 1920s, when this piece was published in the popular magazine, *Now and Then*:

---

[121] Langdon-Davies, p. 116. [122] Ibid. [123] Ibid., p. 117.

[124] For a useful look at sexism in the radical book trade, see chapter in *Rolling our Own: Women as Printers, Publishers, and Distributors*, pp. 99–107. For work on women 'hidden' within publishing, see Rebecca Lyons, 'Thanks for Penguin: Women, Invisible Labour, and Publishing in the Mid-Twentieth Century', in Juliana Dresvina, ed., *Thanks for Typing: Remembering Forgotten Women in History* (London: Bloomsbury, 2021), pp. 50–60; and Elizabeth West, *The Women Who Invented Twentieth-Century Children's Literature* (London: Routledge, 2023).

The future of bookselling is, we believe, likely to be in the hands of well-educated, well-trained women. It is an attractive and suitable career for many who find the professions closely preserved … She must be willing to learn by doing and she must regard the work of dusting, unpacking, wrapping up, looking out from stock, making out bills and giving change as incidental and necessary to her getting a thorough knowledge of the job. Then when she leaves the shop a good portion of her leisure must be devoted to reading. Reading with a purpose. Reading not only books but papers, reviews and catalogues … It is a business which takes the best part of the life of those who work at it and those who succeed in it invariably get to care for it more than for almost any pastime or recognized form of amusement.[125]

The prescience of this editorial was, in fact, anticipated by another in the USA, for *The Atlantic Monthly*, in 1915. Earl Barnes (a past Professor of Education at Stanford University) wrote that bookselling 'would give young women of ability and devotion a wide range of useful exercise for their talents'. He explains:

As industrial agents, they would be handling goods that would make for larger intelligence and for social betterment. They could help individuals and the community at large. The work would be active and varied but not too laborious; and they would be meeting men and women under conditions of freedom and security which might naturally lead to their largest possible life. Even if it did not, it would still be an interesting and useful life, independent of the caprice of directors, and admirably fitted for youth, middle age, and old age.[126]

---

[125] 'Editorial', *Now and Then*, Autumn 1927, No. 25, p. 5.

[126] Earl Barnes, 'A New Profession for Women', *The Atlantic Monthly* (1857–1932) 116, August 1915, p. 34.

Ernest Heffer, distinguished Cambridge bookseller, in a lecture on bookselling given at Stationers' Hall on 11 March 1927, showed the slightly less positive attitude towards women booksellers from within the book trade itself:

> In the first place, he or she (and there is no doubt but that we men, sooner or later, will have to reckon with the competition of women) must possess a good memory for titles.[127]

And in an article written in the same publication in June that year, 'Double U Tee Enn' claims that sales and service by women booksellers

> will never have that 'kick' about it, as when handled by 'a mere man'. There always seems to be 'something' missing . . . sentiment seems to enter into the transaction – gets the better of them – and a sale is not clinched.[128]

This is because in part, he claims, 'a great proportion of the malcontents, of shall we say, indifferent female sales staff, get it into their minds that one day sooner or later, they will meet their "beau ideal," get married, and business need not worry them anymore, as long as they have someone earning for them'.[129]

Even the editor of the time seems to feel this is a criticism too far, though, as at the end of this article there is an editorial intervention, which states that 'We are glad to say that our experience of the female assistant is far more favourable than that of our correspondent. We have often asked the proprietor of a business who employed female assistants how it answered, and found that most of them had no complaint to make or at least no more than they had as regards male assistants.'[130]

---

[127] Recorded in full in *The Publishers' Circular and Booksellers' Record*, 19 March 1927, pp. 343–369.

[128] 'Double U Tee Enn', 'Women and Salesmanship', in *The Publishers' Circular and Booksellers' Record*, 11 June 1927, p. 725.

[129] Ibid. [130] Ibid.

Despite these pieces, however, most books that were written about the book trade during this period appear to ignore the place of women booksellers completely. In *The Book World*, published in 1935 (and then revised and expanded under the new title, *The Book World Today*, in 1957),[131] chapters focussing on bookselling make no mention of a female workforce, ironically despite acknowledging their place in other businesses and the impact this has had upon their status as book-buyers: 'The advent of women in business and the professions has brought a large new element into the book buying public'[132] says J. G. Wilson, omitting to mention what elements women booksellers were also bringing into the trade.[133] By 1935, for example, Christina Foyle had been running her Literary Luncheons for several years, and by 1937, an article about her in the magazine *The Bystander* could claim that she had increased the sales from Foyles from four hundred thousand to around the million mark: 'she has turned the trade upside down, and has started so many successful book clubs that within eighteen months the revenue from them will be twice that of her family's existing business of selling new and second-hand books'.[134] That these achievements did not make it into any of the formal publications of the time which described the book trade illustrates the way histories can be so easily lost, especially those around women.

[131] John Hampden, ed., *The Book World* (London: Thomas Nelson, 1935); and John Hampden, ed., *The Book World Today* (London: George Allen & Unwin Ltd, 1951).

[132] John G. Wilson, 'Bookselling in London', in *Hampden* (1935), p. 124.

[133] Wilson does slightly better in 1945, in *The Business of Bookselling* (London: The Associated Booksellers of Great Britain and Ireland, 1945) when he says in the concluding pages that 'the future of the bookselling trade will depend on an increased number of intelligent men and women who will approach the bookshop as the sphere of their life's work through disciplined experience in routine, literature, and sound business training', p. 74.

[134] Charles Graves, 'More Celebrities in Cameo No 47: Christina Foyle', *The Bystander* 136, 24 November 1937, p. 281.

4 Women Booksellers

In the only text we have which claims to map out the histories of bookselling in Britain covering the twentieth century, *Publishing and Bookselling*, the fifth and sixth editions (which came out in 1974 and 1982, respectively),[135] the presence of women booksellers is acknowledged by Norrie, first like this:

> The 'thirties brought some formidable women into bookselling – besides Miss Santoro, Miss Dillon, Miss Reckitt and Miss Babbidge all made the grade in the man's world of commerce.[136]

And then, in 1982, this has been rewritten to say:

> The immediate pre-war period brought some formidable women into bookselling – Una Dillon, Eva Reckitt, Christina Foyle. Miss Santoro's achievements, regardless of her sex, were those of a pioneer.[137]

It is really striking that the same adjective comes up in describing these women again and again: 'formidable', a word seen earlier attributed to Hilda Light. Analysing the language used reveals a great deal: 'Formidable' is a term that the *OED* defines as meaning something that 'gives cause for fear or alarm'. In French, of course, it means almost the opposite – fabulous, or marvellous, but the meaning here is the English one. This is backed up by this third quotation, from Michael Geare, a publishing sales director in the 1950s, and then editorial director and deputy editor of *The Bookseller*:

[135] I cannot find any reference to women booksellers of the early twentieth century in earlier editions written solely by Mumby.

[136] *Publishing and Bookselling*, 5th Ed., p. 389.

[137] *Publishing and Bookselling in the Twentieth Century*, 6th Ed., p. 84.

> When I came into this business many a man had to pluck up
> his courage to go into a bookshop. There were these daunting
> lady booksellers in ravelled cardigans; intellectual, clever
> women.[138]

'Daunting' and 'ravelled' undercut the final adjectives – the spectre of the
bookish bluestocking, dowdy and single, can clearly be seen. However, as
the following sections will show, these descriptions do not accurately reflect
these women or their accomplishments: and yet these same adjectives crop
up again and again to describe them.

Provincial Booksellers: Elise Santoro, Irene Babbidge, and Margot Heginbothom

The south of England produced some active and successful women booksellers in the mid twentieth century: other parts in the UK, as already
flagged earlier on in this Element, did so too. The three case studies which
follow, however, justify their place here because of their work for the
Booksellers Association as well as their own bookshops: they show extraordinary reach and influence between them, in different and sometimes
overlapping areas.

Elise Santoro

In Tim Waterstone's autobiography, he recalls how important The Book
Club, a bookshop in Crowborough, East Sussex, was to him in his school-
days. This bookshop was run by Miss Elise Santoro, who Waterstone
describes as 'dauntingly severe', even as he credits her for kindling within
him the bookseller vision which then turned into Waterstones:

> Much of Waterstones' inherent values . . . were being tested
> out there by Miss Santoro before my very eyes. The quality
> of her stock range, which . . . was broad and decidedly
> literary in style. Her marketing outreach into the community.
> The comfort and warmth of her shop. Her extraordinary

[138] Michael Geare, quoted in *The British Book Trade: An Oral History*, p. 107.

> personal knowledge about books and their quality and their
> titles and their authors, and her enthusiasm for promoting her
> favourites.[139]

Considering the commanding position Waterstones now holds in book-selling, Elise Santoro's impact within the book trade is definitely worth further research. Her obituary in *The Bookseller* highlights her long service to the Booksellers Association, whose Council she served on for over twenty years: she was a regular attender at the annual conferences, her comments at which are 'remembered as both cogent and pungent'. These odd choices of adjectives are coupled with a statement that she ran her bookshop 'successfully and indomitably' until she was in her eighties, when she retired in 1973. And, of course, the very first adjective in this obituary to describe her is 'formidable' – she was a 'formidable but greatly liked trade figure'.[140]

Miss Santoro was active in the Booksellers Association, both at Branch level (she was Chair between 1959 and 1961, acted as Branch member for the BA Council, and was given honorary life membership on her retirement) and via the national committee, serving on different Boards such as the Examination Board, the National Book League Committee, and the Education Board. She was a frequent guest lecturer at bookseller training events: *The Bookseller* notes her giving a paper on 'Contemporary Fiction' at the Havant Bookselling School in both 1955 and 1956.[141] She was also part of the group called the 'Friends of Tallies', set up in 1950 to try and save the Book Tally scheme, which operated to provide a children's version of Book Tokens, but which ultimately failed after a few years because of combination of paper shortages, manufacturing and tax issues.[142] Her name crops up frequently in reports of the annual BA conferences, where it is possible to get a strong sense of her personality and outspokenness

---

[139] Tim Waterstone, *The Face Pressed up against the Window* (London: Atlantic Books, 2019), p. 42.

[140] 'Elise Santoro', *The Bookseller*, 9 October 1982, p. 1373.

[141] See *The Bookseller*, 26 February 1955, p. 856; and *The Bookseller*, 14 April 1956, p. 1046.

[142] More work on this scheme to follow in a separate paper.

about issues she believed in, like Book Tokens and Book Tallies.[143] In 1966, for instance, when the designs of Book Token cards were discussed in Southport, it is Miss Santoro who seconds a motion to increase the number of options available, and who asks the Chairman of Book Tokens, Mr Schollick, why they cannot do one of a horse, cat, dog, or bird. Schollick points out that there is one with a dog on it, and shows it to her: 'Why can't you give me one which looks *happy*?' she is reported as replying. 'Clearly, Mr Schollick indicated, Book Tokens could not win',[144] – not, as this incident shows, when dealing with a bookseller who knows what her customers want and is not afraid to fight for it. Santoro's advocacy for her fellow booksellers can be seen again and again in *Bookseller* reports: in 1960, attending a Commercial Libraries Group meeting organised by the Booksellers Association, and hearing that the libraries were putting out a leaflet trying to persuade people to subscribe to their lending services, she is recorded as protesting that the phrase 'There's no need to buy that book' needed to be taken out.[145]

When Santoro's shop moved premises in 1968, Ross Higgins, the President of the Booksellers Association at the time, summarised her achievements:

> It was the bookseller's job to bring book and reader together. In this Miss Santoro had been outstandingly successful. She knew, through long experience, her own public extremely well; her eclectic taste and sound judgement had led her customers to trust her implicitly. Because of this she had built up, and kept in being, despite the increasingly adverse circumstances of the times, an intensely personal bookshop where the customers' book requirements were the prime consideration.[146]

---

[143] Book Tallies were a short-lived scheme, aimed at children. Costing sixpence each, they worked like book tokens but were designed so that children could buy and collect them.

[144] 'Clippers or Dogs?', *The Bookseller*, 21 May 1966, p. 2260.

[145] See 'Commercial Libraries Decide to Speak up for Themselves', *The Bookseller*, 12 March 1960, p. 1276.

[146] Ross Higgins, quoted in *The Bookseller*, 21 September 1968, p. 949.

Ian Norrie underlines her importance by saying that 'few, if any, small towns in the whole of Britain had a bookshop with as comprehensive a stock as Miss Santoro's, or were owned by anyone as compulsively dedicated to her task'.[147] That is quite an accolade for someone who took over the Book Club in the early 1930s with no experience of the trade, in partnership with one Miss Frampton (still a shadowy figure in the archives). By 1939 they had established a library delivery service over an eight-mile radius, and had branches in Mayfield and Uckfield, too.[148] Note how Norrie frames both of his pieces on women booksellers at the start of this section using Santoro as the key lead figure: she was, 'regardless of her sex, a pioneer' because she proved wrong Basil Blackwell's pronouncement that no bookshop could survive in a non-university town of less than forty thousand people.[149] He praised her approach to bookselling which came from a love of literature, remaining 'remarkably unsullied' during her time running The Book Club, something 'that cannot be said of some whose standards wilted a little in the pursuit of a comfortable livelihood'.[150]

Irene Babbidge

Ian Norrie's sometimes erratic approach to history can be seen in the two short extracts at the beginning of this section from different editions of *Publishing and Bookselling*. Names have been redistributed: in the passage from the 1982 edition, Irene Babbidge has been deleted, but she is mentioned elsewhere in the same volume as one of two 'formidable' women booksellers in Hampshire.[151]

Miss Babbidge's bookselling career began in 1931 in Stoneham's shop in London's Cheapside. Here she studied for and completed a three-year Diploma in Bookselling, then added commercial lending library work to her portfolio, before starting the Ibis Library, in Banstead, Surrey, with Evelyn Folds-Taylor

---

[147] *Publishing and Bookselling*, 5th Ed., p. 551. [148] Ibid., p. 389.

[149] See *Publishing and Bookselling in the Twentieth Century*, 6th Ed, p. 84, and Basil Blackwell, 'Provincial Bookselling', in John Hampden, ed., *The Book World: A New Survey* (London: Thomas Nelson & Sons, 1935), pp. 134–149.

[150] *Publishing and Bookselling in the Twentieth Century*, 6th Ed, p. 84.

[151] Ibid., p. 202.

in 1938. She then started another in 1941 in Havant, called the Pelham Library, and in 1951 The Bay Tree Bookshop in Waterlooville, Hampshire. Soon after this, she went to Paris for six months to work at La Hune, a bookshop 'right in the midst of the artistic and literary quarter of that city', making her 'one of the few members of the trade who, in addition to many years bookselling experience in this country, also has a first-hand knowledge of the French book trade'.[152] It is presumably this love of travel, and interest in international bookselling (she mentions going to a meeting with booksellers from France, Germany, Italy, Holland, Belgium and Austria, in a piece about bookseller training in 1959)[153] which helps provide the motivation for successfully getting the funding to allow bookselling assistants to go to international schools of bookselling and to establish a Publishers Continental Bookshop Awards.[154]

Her standing within the book trade was such that, in July 1962, she was chosen to be a witness in defence of the Net Book Agreement in front of the Restrictive Practices Court: this case was a significant battle won by a close collaboration between the Booksellers' and Publishers' Associations, and Babbidge was picked as one of the twenty-five people to give evidence, one of four booksellers to take the stand. The account of the case reveals much about Babbidge's bookselling practice – and the respect in which she was held at the time, throughout the book trade. In the introduction, John Boon, President of the Publishers Association, noted that the witnesses were very carefully chosen, and singled out Babbidge, who he said 'made perhaps the most forceful and telling appearance in the witness box'.[155] This claim is supported by comments captured from W. A. Bagnall, Q.C.:

---

[152] 'Meet the Bookseller: Irene Babbidge', in *The Publishers Circular and Booksellers Record*, 13 September 1958, p. 1201.

[153] Irene Babbidge, 'An Enterprise Much Admired', *The Bookseller*, 21 February 1959, p. 983.

[154] Referenced in 'Change of Chairman for the Education Board', *Bookshop*, August–September 1961, p. 82.

[155] John Boon, 'Introduction', in *Books Are Different: An Account of the Defence of the Net Book Agreement before the Restrictive Practices Court in 1962*, eds. R. E. Barker and G. R. Davies (London: Macmillan, 1966), p. 50.

The Court saw her giving her evidence and, I would submit, could properly have been very impressed with her both as a witness and as the proprietress of a bookshop. She was dedicated to her work and to serving the public. I remember and have noted one or two of her answers which were, I submit to the Court, most impressive on this part of the case. The Court will remember the case of the gas-worker who started to use Miss Babbidge's shop and she interested him in books on various subjects and she helped him to build up a small library of books . . . He started as a book borrower and became a book buyer, and profited by this service.

Bagnall also notes Babbidge's indignation when it was suggested to her that the only people who were interested in cultural books were middle-class, and her concerns about the impact dropping some of her current methods of operation would have on her customers:

I should feel that I had let them down. There are people in the New Town whom we have converted to being bookshop customers. I would not worry so much about the people in the old town, because they are bookshop customers already and would find somewhere else to buy their books; but I would be concerned with people in the new town, because at the moment they know they can buy a book on any subject and they get help and sympathetic advice, and those people I think would be bereft.[156]

She is also mentioned in the Justice's judgement:

Miss Babbidge, who is managing director of a bookshop in Havant, is clearly most anxious to win customers from among the inhabitants of the neighbouring new town of Leigh Park, not merely because she regards it as a mission to encourage

---

[156] *Books Are Different*, pp. 840–841.

such potential customers to become readers of books and of
as wide and worthy a selection of literature as possible. As
a bookseller she takes a keen personal interest in the individual tastes of her customers ... this sense of personal voca-
tion, which is undoubtedly valuable to the public, may well
account for many booksellers remaining in business notwith-
standing that their profits are modest ...[157]

All these points link back to those earlier discussions by critics and the book
trade about the value of the bookshop in building new readers, and in
guiding and supporting their choices. Babbidge spoke as witness with
conviction and with professional confidence, and in the transcript of her
evidence, a bookseller of experience and commitment clearly emerges. In
the press she is described as a 'dedicated and efficient small town bookseller
and one of the most effective witnesses on behalf of the Net Book
Agreement in the Restrictive Practices Court in 1962'.[158] Yet despite, as
she reveals, having had bookselling roles in London, Paris, Brighton,
Banstead, Waterlooville and Havant, being a member of the Education
Board of the Booksellers Association since 1954, (and Chairman from 1956
to 1961), actively engaged in lecturing to trainees under the Board's
education scheme, a correspondence course tutor in Bookshop Practice
and Bookshop Management, and a member of the Booksellers Association
Council,[159] she is reduced to being 'the lady bookseller of Havant' in Gerry
Davies's account of the Net Book Agreement case.[160] John Hyams's
reflections on his life as a bookseller are more emphatically complimentary:
her 'feisty performance' before the judge had made her a 'trade heroine',[161]

[157] Ibid., p. 13.
[158] 'Selling Books', *The Times Literary Supplement*, 13 May 1965, p. 380.
[159] See Babbidge's recorded statement in *Books Are Different*, p. 258.
[160] Gerry Davies was a librarian before becoming the General Secretary of the
Booksellers Association (1955–1965). This quote from him comes from *The
British Book Trade: An Oral History*, p. 174.
[161] John Hyams, 'First Person: Ruminations of a Career in British Bookselling
1949–1988', in *Logos* 19/2 2008, p. 81.

he claims. And Rayner Unwin, President of the Publishers Association, speaking at her retirement party in Brighton in 1971, recalled and celebrated her court appearance: 'Irene Babbidge stood at the wicket and scored runs against the wickedest fast bowling that ever came the way of anyone in the book trade ... that's why no small bookseller in the trade has earned so much respect than she.'[162]

In 1964, *The Bookseller* published the text of a paper Miss Babbidge gave in Paris at a meeting of the International Community of Booksellers' Associations, entitled 'Some Obstacles in the Way',[163] which restates her commitment to the Net Book Agreement, and for fixed prices, so that international collaboration on the free movement of books could take place. She talks authoritatively and eloquently about the impact price-cutting would have on bookshops like hers, which operated outside of the big cities:

> What would happen if the supermarket, which is across the street from my shop, were able to cut prices on bestsellers? ... The fact is that more than half of the stock of my shop would be susceptible to price-cutting and I should have to reduce very considerably my ordering of books, both prior to publication and for replacement of basic stock sold. Ultimately I should cease to be a stock holding bookseller and I should at least have to curtail my trading activities, if I did not go out of business altogether.[164]

The other challenge to prices would be if consumer tax were to be applied to books, she says: something which British books were (and still are) exempt from, unlike many other European countries. Despite the fact that this battle was fought with the government during the war, and was won, demonstrating,

---

[162] Rayner Unwin, quoted in 'Farewell Party for Irene Babbidge', *The Bookseller*, 26 June 1971, p. 2592.

[163] Irene Babbidge, 'Some Obstacles in the Way', *The Bookseller*, 20 June 1964, pp. 2222–2224.

[164] Ibid., p. 2223.

Babbidge says, 'that fundamentally "books are different"', it is still necessary to keep a focus on the danger of new attempts to impose taxes.[165] She points to the recent implementation of such a tax in Ireland, bookending her earlier reference to a bill going through Parliament calling for the abolition of all resale price maintenance forms.[166] The fragility of the situation is emphasised: though the Publishers Association has made petitions to the government, pointing out the huge amount of money (over £35,000) already spent on the defence of the Net Book Agreement in 1962, and the Minister's promise that he will consider providing a clause to cover cases like books, Babbidge calls attention to the 'meagre comfort' this is for the British book trade.[167] She is fiercely protective of the role of the stockholding bookseller, and there is further evidence of this in *The Bookseller*, for instance a little later in 1964, when, at the BA Conference in Gleneagles she is quoted as attacking a new mailorder book scheme, Bookplan, when the speaker, one Norman Lonsdale, claimed that it would not impact on book sales in bookshops, and would, in fact, help bring more people into these spaces. Miss Babbidge was unconvinced:

> Mr Lonsdale was hitting booksellers below the belt. She read extracts from the Bookplan prospectus, which laid its chief emphasis on the fact that books were at 'far below their usual shop prices' and represented 'savings of 40 per cent on retail prices'. That was not going to send people into bookshops, she said.[168]

In addition to her advocacy work at national and international level on matters of book prices and where books were sold, she was clearly a creative and effective teacher: in 1956, at one of the series of successful bookselling courses she instigated for booksellers in the South of England, her publicised lecture on book trade education was given as a one-act play, which she had written herself. The play showed 'the way in which a bookshop should be conducted by the staff in the absence of the proprietor'.[169] The

[165] Ibid., p. 2224. [166] Ibid., p. 2222. [167] Ibid.

[168] 'Selling Books as Bargains', *The Bookseller*, 27 June 1964, p. 2278.

[169] 'One Day School in Brighton', *The Bookseller*, 14 April 1956, p. 1046.

play, 'On a February Morning', is published in full in *The Bookseller*, and manages to pack in many examples of how to manage various customer requests, via the characters of Betty Jackson (junior assistant) and Helen Sharp (senior assistant), as they manage Makepeace & Co whilst their manager is out at a country house library sale.[170] They deal with customer orders, highlighting the issues of incomplete bibliographic details (or incorrect ones) sent by the customers, and the importance of factoring in realistic postal charges, so as not to erode any profit margin. They also tackle the issue of bad packing by publishers, and discounts and support for school orders, via the character of Mr Yorke, 'the eccentric headmaster of a local school', and help a customer looking for a children's book for a child sick with the chicken-pox (a space-ship press-out book and three Puffins are chosen) and another looking for a book for her boyfriend's mother (a book on dogs is suggested and welcomed). Alongside all of this activity (and the prerequisite dusting, which Betty is engaged with at the start of the morning), Babbidge draws in mention of Net books, new titles and the importance of not displaying these until publication day, the courtesy of sharing stock with a neighbouring bookseller when needed, and a reminder that the school order will have to be packed as luggage, as a taxi cannot carry goods.[171] There is humour as well as detail in this short piece, and as a 'painless method of revision'[172] showcases Babbidge's engagement with junior staff training.

Babbidge's work around bookseller training and education resulted in a book, *Beginning in Bookselling*, which sold so well the first edition, which came out in 1965, was revised and republished in 1972.[173] The foreword was written by Basil Blackwell, who praised its merits for being in inverse ratio to its bulk, saying 'every page is compact of wisdom drawn from experience'[174] and a review in the *Sunday Telegraph* claimed it has 'everything the tyro bookseller needs to know ... is lucidly outlined ... and there

---

[170] Irene Babbidge, 'Revision without Tears: "On a February Morning"', *The Bookseller*, 2 June 1956, pp. 1502–1503.

[171] Ibid. [172] Ibid., p. 1502.

[173] Irene Babbidge, *Beginning in Bookselling* (London: Andre Deutsch, 1965).

[174] Basil Blackwell, 'Foreword'; ibid., p. 7.

are few members of the book-buying or the book-selling public who could not benefit from reading it'.[175] Perhaps ironically, this review is alongside one for Thomas Joy's *The Truth About Bookselling*, which is 'equally to be recommended' in its 'much more detailed way'.[176]

The Bookseller published extracts from the first edition, and prefaces these with a description of Miss Babbidge as not only having appeared so 'admirably and effectively' in court, but who also still helped out with the packing of parcels in her shop. This, and her experience as past Chair of the Education Board, and now with this book, showed that she was 'fully alive to the vital importance of intelligent service if the independent bookseller is to survive'.[177]

In the 1958 article about her in the *Publishers Circular and Booksellers Record*, already mentioned above, she was summarised as a bookseller who was 'not only an astute businesswoman, but who has the interest of the Trade truly at heart'.[178] Thirteen years later Eric Bailey, the President of the Booksellers Association, lamented the fact that several years ago, because of business and health reasons, she had had to withdraw from the office of vice-presidency. *The Bookseller* quotes him as saying he was one of the many people who had looked forward to her being the Association's first woman president.[179] In her obituary in *The Bookseller* in 1983, Gerry Davies also mentions this, saying:

> It was the hope of her contemporaries that she would go on to be president; sadly, her conscientious attention to her own business made it impossible for her to attain an office she richly deserved and for which she had all the qualities and capability. She had to choose between becoming the BA's first woman president or remaining an active personal bookseller, and in elegant ladylike fashion she told me 'I would rather be thought of as a bookseller in my own right.'[180]

[175] Tom Manwaring, in 'All Set for Romance', *Sunday Telegraph*, 7 March 1965, p. 21.
[176] Ibid. [177] 'Making a Good Start', in *The Bookseller*, 16 January 1965, p. 116.
[178] 'Meet the Bookseller: Irene Babbidge', in *The Publishers Circular and Booksellers Record*, 13 September 1958, p. 1201.
[179] 'Farewell Party for Irene Babbidge', *The Bookseller*, 26 June 1971, p. 2592.
[180] Gerry Davies, 'Irene Babbidge', *The Bookseller*, 2 April 1983, p. 1236.

For all these reasons, she should have a visible place in British bookselling history. Norrie has dropped all mention of her place in the Restrictive Practices Court in the sixth edition of *Publishing and Bookselling*, and even in the fifth edition, she is just one of a list of names, with no clue given to her key part in the proceedings.[181]

Margot Heginbothom

The third bookseller from the south of England I chose to highlight is Margot Heginbothom (who became Margot Tyrie when she married in 1953). Her history is even more obscured than the two which precede it, but her achievements, complementary and also distinct from her peers make it no less valuable a study. After an apprenticeship in Bath, she joined F. J. Ward's London bookshop in 1933, and was then sent, four years later, to the Brighton branch, which she ran until Frank Ward and Kenneth Bredon returned from the war. In a short article in *The Bookseller*, in 1944, the ways she coped with 'the stressed and strains' of the war years have, it was claimed, 'revealed her as one of the outstanding young booksellers in the country today'.[182] Indeed, this can be seen from evidence found in the pages of *The Bookseller*: in 1943 the text of a paper she read at the annual conference of what was then still the Associated Booksellers, entitled 'The Bookshop and the Community', appeared.[183] In this she sets out her arguments for why bookshops are central to their communities, beginning with a statement explaining what has gone wrong:

> I have a reputation for stepping in where angels fear to tread ... but I would suggest that our trouble is partly due to the fact that we have had to struggle so hard to make a bookshop pay its way, let alone make a profit, that we have lost our sense of proportion. Books have become commodities. Terms and turnover have become increasingly important, and

---

[181] *Publishing and Bookselling*, 5th Ed., p. 436.

[182] Frank J. Ward, *The Bookseller*, 27 July 1944, p. 40.

[183] Margot Heginbothom, 'The Bookshop and the Community' in *The Bookseller*, 8 July 1943, pp. 18–21.

> before the war most of us gave space in our shops willingly
> enough to sidelines to eke out the meagre profits which accrued
> from the sale of books. A grievous state of affairs, for if we are
> booksellers surely we should sell books, not rubber ducks,
> handbags or tubes of paint.[184]

Her paper is an exposition of the responsibilities she stresses the booksellers have: to 'establish our priceless literary heritage in this generation'; to fulfil the needs of the community by ensuring books on a wide range of subjects are available; and to 'reflect daily events, and in some measure the history of our own time'. The bookshop, she stresses, should be an accessible educational space, where children and young people are actively encouraged to visit, via competitions, invitations to Youth Groups, and dedicated Children's Book Weeks.[185] In addition, booksellers should 'co-operate much more closely with the various progressive movements, with the public libraries ... and with the Churches', and not forget they have responsibilities to publishers, because booksellers are the 'connecting link between them and the public', and to those who are following on in bookselling: she suggests that any bookseller who has been in the trade for three years should be given the chance to complete a three- or six-month course, 'to gain a wider and deeper knowledge of the trade and of literature'.[186]

Heginbothom's final section is frank about the need for publishers to stop supplying places where books are not the primary item for sale: several years after Margaret Cole's articles underlining the link between education and people's apprehension around entering bookshops, and only one year after the Mass Observation project showed the dearth of bookshops in many areas of the country, it is clear not much has changed:

> The public before the war was by no means bookshop
> conscious. Many people seemed too awestruck to darken
> our doors. Before now I have been asked in a frightened
> voice if we sold books. Others, less timid, have expected us
> to sell anything and everything. I have had requests for

[184] Ibid., p. 18.   [185] Ibid., p.18–19.   [186] Ibid., p. 20.

> stamps, cigarettes, sandwich tickets and domestic servants
> and a variety of other things in Brighton. It is astonishing
> how few people use bookshops.[187]

Her suggestion for how this can be improved is to finish with a request that more information be collected on consumers and how they view books and bookshops – an idea which, she would be pleased to know, is now a key tool for booksellers today, as consumer insight underpins marketing books to readers.

Heginbothom's paper was judged 'a stimulating and progressive expression of opinion' by the conference – and of such importance that it was given time at the expense of another scheduled paper on 'Discount to Public Libraries'.[188] Her voice is heard again later that same year, when another talk she gave, this time to the London Branch, is published in full in *The Bookseller* in September 1943. Heginbothom acknowledges the privilege, saying:

> If ever I wore a hat, its size today would be extra large OS.
> Twice in the last three months the Association has paid me
> a very great compliment, first asking me to speak at the
> Conference last June, and now asking me to address this
> meeting of the London Branch.[189]

This second paper takes 'The Small Bookseller after the War' as its focus, and showcases Heginbothom's skill in pulling together historical parallels with current events to expose similarities and differences of the book trade. The paper showed how bookselling had coped with events such as the Great Fire of London in 1666 in the past, when, just as in 1940, the centre of the book world was destroyed. The Star Chamber's censorship of publications in 1637 were, she points out, far worse than those imposed in 1943, but she does use this allusion to point out that the Star Chamber's decrees did

---

[187] Ibid., p. 20. [188] 'Post War Problems', *The Bookseller*, 1 July 1943, p. 5.
[189] Margot Heginbothom, 'The Small Bookseller after the War', *The Bookseller*, 16 September 1943, p. 287.

include a prohibition on any other kind of tradesperson apart from a bookseller to sell books – something, as has already been seen from her earlier lecture, she wants to see stricter regulations about in her time.[190] It is noteworthy that she refutes the part of this decree which said a bookseller had to be apprenticed to another for seven years before they could do business themselves, though, using this as an opportunity to point out that 'two excellent bookshops in Sussex started and run by women who had had no previous experience in the trade prove that such rigidity is unnecessary today'.[191] Frustratingly, she does not name these women, although the implication that her London-based audience will know who these are makes the assumption that one of these, at least, is Elise Santoro.

In the following year another article, 'Orders in Uniform', appeared; in this one Miss Heginbothom proposed a simple solution to the problem of keeping tabs on orders to publishers: 'tear out all the duplicate orders from the [order] book, and file them alphabetically under publisher, and in date order'.[192] She then goes on to suggest a template for a new order form, which has been put together after extensive consultation with publishers, travellers, trade managers and other booksellers.[193] Heginbothom's authority in speaking on such issues is later confirmed when she is made Chair of the Booksellers Association Education Board, as well as Chair of the Sussex Branch, at the start of the 1950s. As Chair of the Education Board, she oversaw the introduction of correspondence courses for booksellers, as well as a suite of lecture-based courses via branches of the Association where need was identified:

> The education of assistants is the vital concern of every member of the Booksellers Association who is here today. It is for all of us to see that new entrants to the trade have the opportunity to learn the art of bookselling. The apprenticeship system is a thing of the past, and in consequence our

[190] Ibid.　[191] Ibid.

[192] Margot Henginbothom, 'Orders in Uniform', *The Bookseller*, 9 March 1944, p. 282.

[193] Ibid., p. 283.

individual responsibility is lessened; but our corporate
responsibility is correspondingly increased.[194]

Like Irene Babbidge and Elise Santoro, Heginbothom threw herself into
improving the life of the bookseller with commitment and action. An
obituary notes that she was 'an excellent organiser and a most accomplished
speaker'.[195] And yet, despite all this, she is only mentioned once in all of the
editions of *Publishing and Bookselling*, and then only in the 1974 version, in
an unembellished statement connecting her to K. J. Bredon's bookshop.[196]

Radical Bookshops: Eva Collet Reckitt and Margaret Mynatt

The growth of radical bookshops during this period was greatly impacted
by two London women booksellers: Eva Collet Reckitt and Margaret
Mynatt. As Elen Cocaign remarks: 'the decisive role of booksellers as
political and cultural mediators remains largely unexplored',[197] and these
two women certainly showcase these mediating roles.

Eva Collet Reckitt

Eva Collet Reckitt, mentioned by Norrie (see start of this section) as one of
his 'formidable' women booksellers, took over what was known as 'The
Bomb Shop', a political bookshop in Charing Cross Road, in 1934, and
turned it into a highly successful purveyor of revolutionary, socialist, and
progressive publications. She funded the bookshop venture via her Reckitt
and Colman fortune, and was managing director until 1939, and after that its
chairman. She was assisted by another founding director, Olive Netta
Parsons, a former student at Girton College, Cambridge and then the
London School of Economics.

---

[194] Margot Heginbothom, quoted in 'The Work of the Education Board', *The
Bookseller*, 10 June 1950, p. 1194.

[195] Kenneth Bredon, 'Margot Tyrie', *The Bookseller*, 9 June 1984, p. 2321.

[196] *Publishing and Bookselling*, 5th Ed., p. 550.

[197] Elen Cocaign, 'The Left's Bibliophilia in Interwar Britain: Assessing
Booksellers' Role in the Battle of Ideas', *Twentieth Century Communism*, 4,
annual 2012, p. 221.

Reckitt was a graduate of University College London, gaining a first-class honours degree in Philosophy in 1924, and was briefly a part-time lecturer in the department there before leaving to focus on work with the Labour Research Department. Despite these impressive qualifications, in an obituary for Parsons written by John Prime in 1996, the women were described as 'two charming middle-aged women, well-spoken and fashionably dressed' who 'graced' London Branch meetings of the Booksellers Association in the 1930s and 1940s: 'others present were often taken aback by the way their conversation would turn to politics, revealing sympathies far left of the centre'.[198]

Collets was an important early outlet for Victor Gollancz's Left Book Club editions, and was also known for stocking extensive Russian, East European and Chinese publications. Early success resulted in several more Collet's bookshops being started in the provinces – and although these were to disappear again in the 1950s, other initiatives, like a Russian bookshop, a folk record shop, and travelling bookshops, helped ensure continued growth, and in 1976 the business could claim to be a multi-million pound business with a staff of 120.[199]

At a 25th anniversary lunch in 1959, Professor J. D. Bernal credited Collet's for opening a vital window onto the world: 'This window faces mostly East, but there is a great deal that this country now knows which would not have been known had it not been for Collet's.'[200] Another article celebrating this anniversary, written by Reckitt, says that 'the purpose of all these activities and behind the running of the shops themselves was to enlarge the reading public and to bring in the folk who did not ordinarily patronise bookshops, because they seemed too "posh" and expensive'.[201]

---

[198] John Prime, 'Olive Parsons, Director of Collets Bookshops', *The Bookseller*, 17 May 1996, p. 12.

[199] Mark Crail, 'Fifty Years of Collets', *Tribune*, 29 March 1984, p. 2.

[200] Collet's 25th Anniversary Lunch, *The Publishers Circular and Booksellers Record*, 25 April 1959, p. 281.

[201] Eva Collet Reckitt, 'Twenty-Five Years in Charing Cross Road', *The Bookseller*, 21 March 1959, p. 1255.

The National Archives holds files that prove Reckitt was closely monitored by the Secret Service because of her close links with the Communist Party of Great Britain,[202] but this did not deter her from remaining loyal to it and socialism for the rest of her life. Reading these files, and realising the extent of the intrusion (phone calls tapped, letters opened, and even, on at least one occasion, houses searched[203]) is to appreciate the challenging contexts Reckitt was working in, but also to see the generosity she showed to various people asking for loans, which letters reveal as a frequent occurrence.

However, when Collet's moved premises next to Foyles in Charing Cross Road in 1976, under the headline 'Red Eva Moves in on Foyles', Reckitt herself stressed that success was less to do with the radical and political materials the shop was famous for, but more to do with the paperback revolution, which had brought books to a much wider reading public: 'that, despite what they say, was the revolution the owner of the "red" shop was really interested in'.[204] Indeed, Reckitt was an early supporter of Allan Lane's Penguin Books, stocking them from the start, and then opening the first London shop dedicated to them in 1962. A picture in *The Bookseller* taken at this event stresses 'the long record of co-operation between the two firms',[205] and another showing the 25th anniversary

---

[202] The National Archive (TNA): KV 2/1375, KV 2/1370, KV 2/1369, KV 2/ 1372, KV 2/1373, KV 2/1371, KV 2/1374.

[203] See KV 2/1374, a memo from the West Sussex Constabulary dated 18 December 1940. The Hollow, a cottage in Houghton, West Sussex, that Eva Collet Reckitt shared ownership of, and where she was, at that time, spending Friday to Monday of each week, was searched after a tip off from a guest there, one Frederick Head. The search was conducted on Tuesday, 17 December – one of the days Miss Reckitt would not have been on site. The report describes how 'the house is full of communist literature', and how a copy of Miss Reckitt's will had been found in a cabinet, with bequests in it to a number of other known communists. There are no documents in the file which give any indication of any actions following this search, and the subsequent report.

[204] Lesley Adamson, 'Red Eva Moves in on Foyles', *The Guardian*, 23 August 1976, p. 9.

[205] Text under photograph in *The Bookseller*, 30 June 1962, p. 2350.

luncheon shows Reckitt and Lane sitting next to each other.[206] Reckitt makes reference to the support Collet's received from other key publishers of the 1930s – Sir Stanley Unwin, Victor Gollancz, Sir Francis Meynell and W. G. Taylor, of Dent's – and admits that at the start, 'the whole affair was a triumph of hope over inexperience'. The advice these men gave, as well as the time of the bookshop's opening in the 1930s, 'when the young were anxious to read and study – even to buy'[207] helped make the bookshop a success.

When Eva Collet Reckitt died, very soon after the new premises of Collet's next to Foyles were opened, there were obituaries in outlets as varied as *The Times* and *History Workshop*: 'a kindly and generous person with a streak of shrewd termination and a refreshing candour about accepted institutions'[208] was one summary. 'Shrewd and realistic but [without] a trace of cynicism ... her socialism was a living thing, a matter of thought, criticism and conviction, as well as of the personal loyalties nourished by a lifetime's activity', reads another.[209] *The Bookseller* notes that 'it is not often that a bookseller rates the top position in *The Times* obituaries';[210] that Eva Collet Reckitt received this mark of esteem illustrates her impact on many areas of British intellectual and cultural life. A bookshop, as noted Marxist economist Maurice Dobbs claimed, which:

> had made a very real contribution to the study of linguistics, literature and science of those two great and still little-understood nations of the world, China and the Soviet Union; they had been pioneers, and in future decades, when those studies were more advanced than they were now, the contribution of the bookshop would be recognised as being of signal importance.[211]

[206] 'Collet's 25th Anniversary Luncheon', *The Bookseller*, 25 April 1959, p. 1549.

[207] Reckitt, 'Twenty-Five Years in Charing Cross Road', p. 1254.

[208] 'Miss Eva Reckitt', *The Times*, 28 September 1976, p. 18.

[209] R. E. S., 'Eva Reckitt', *History Workshop*, 2, Autumn 1976, p. 239.

[210] 'Eva Reckitt', *The Bookseller*, 2 October 1976, p. 1996.

[211] 'Collet's 25th Anniversary Luncheon', p. 1549.

Margaret (Bianca) Mynatt

Margaret Mynatt, who was the manager of Central Books between 1952 and 1966, is another bookseller who was part of the Communist party; she was also editor in chief of the collected works of Marx and Engels, and the publisher of the first collected works of Brecht. The trail to find information about her was challenging, but it is hoped that this small section here will inspire further work, as she is a key figure to compare to Eva Collet Reckitt. Central Books, as a distributor of books and magazines for the Communist Party and other left-wing organisations and publishers, is still going strong, now based in Chadwell Heath, in East London. It was officially registered in 1939, and the first small shop opened in late 1941, at 2 Parton Street, London, sharing premises with the publisher Lawrence and Wishart.[212] In the decade which followed, Lawrence and Wishart moved premises, and Central Books expanded, not only next door into 4 Parton Street, but into storage space in Charlotte Street, Southampton Place, and Great James Street, while the warehouse moved to 1 Doughty Street in November 1945.[213] By the time Mynatt became managing director in 1952, Central Books had weathered some hard-hitting political and financial storms, and she oversaw another period of huge change: the Suez Canal crisis and then the uprising in Hungary had a big impact on foreign sales, and the ongoing Cold War hit sales at home, with the manager reporting 'a steep decline in sales to District Bookshops (mainly London and the Home Counties)' and in August 1957 'a very serious position' because of the further decline in sales, the collapse of an arrangement for imports from Russia, and a drying up of orders from China, as well as increased overheads.[214]

There is evidence in the National Archives that she was being closely monitored during the period she managed Central Books by the Secret

---

[212] For more on the book trade activity in Parton Street, see Matthew Chambers, *London and the Modernist Bookshop* (Cambridge: Cambridge University Press, 2020).

[213] See Dave Cope, *Central Books: A Brief History 1939 to 1999* (London: Central Books Ltd, 1999).

[214] Ibid., p. 26.

Service: files contain transcripts of telephone conversations, copies of letters, and other materials relating to her activity during this period.[215] In one report from 1956, from the Special Branch of the Metropolitan Police, there is this negatively framed description of her:

> Medium build; shapeless figure; hair brown; complexion ruddy (apparently effected by cosmetics); large nose; flat-footed; thick ankles. Occasionally wears spectacles.[216]

Perhaps given the nature of these documents, it is not surprising that the descriptions found here about Mynatt are frequently negative – although the transcriptions from her colleagues give an overall impression of someone who could be challenging to deal with, had bouts of serious illness, and who liked to travel, with evidence of trips to Russia and China in the files. She was 'the most emotional woman and had "the most wild enthusiasms"', according to Communist party worker Betty Reid,[217] and could be 'an incorrigible and born intriguer'.[218] James Klugman, head of the Communist Party's Education Department, is quoted as saying she was 'deceitful, double-crossing, conniving, impossible'[219] but the evidence from these documents is also of a woman constantly on the move, dedicated to her cause, and not afraid to speak her mind.

She is described as 'devoted, totally committed, and conscientious' and 'as slightly on the authoritarian side' in Dave Cope's history of Central Books:[220] she does not appear at all in any of the editions of Mumby's and Norrie's *Publishing and Bookselling*, and she is only name-checked once in *The British Book Trade: An Oral History*, where she (significantly) appears in a list of

---

[215] See The National Archives (TNA): KV 2/ 3365 and KV 2/3366.

[216] KV 2/ 3365: Metropolitan Police, Special Branch Report, 16 April 1956, p. 2.

[217] KV 2 /3365, Extract dated 16th February 1953. Comment attributed to Betty Reid.

[218] KV 2/3366, Extract dated 30th March 1960. Comment attributed to John Gollan.

[219] KV 2/3366, Extract dated 22nd March 1960. Comment attributed to James Klugman.

[220] Cope, p. 25.

other women booksellers (Christina Foyle, Una Dillon, Elizabeth Weiler, and Gerti Kvergic) in a comment by Maureen Condon, who ran bookshops in King's Lynn with John Prime between 1968 and 1982. Condon makes the point that 'these women were never part of the boys' club, but they obviously ran bookshops which were excellent in every way'.[221] Neither is Mynatt mentioned in *The Bookseller* (apart from a couple of small pieces regarding Central Books events), so although Central Books were members of the Booksellers Association, it does not look like she was a regular attender at events in the way the other booksellers in this study were.

And yet, as her obituary in *The Times* emphasises, 'she worked, with wisdom and impressive executive talent, in journalism and publishing; at Reuters, as head of Soviet Monitor (1941–51), as manager of Central Books and finally as a director of Lawrence and Wishart'.[222] In 1997, a posthumous publication of the work she wrote with Yvonne Kapp in 1940, appeared.[223] *British Policy and the Refugees, 1933–41* deals with the internment of refugees who suddenly became 'enemy aliens' as the War involved more countries in Europe, and who were deported to countries like Canada and Australia. The book has been hailed as 'highly polemical' and 'an historical document of great interest',[224] and the foreword by Charmian Brinson stresses the great work Mynatt did in setting up the British Committee for Refugees from Czechoslovakia in 1938, quoting a contemporary as saying she was 'the heart and soul of our entire enterprise'.[225] She was then dismissed from this job in 1940, as the internment process was set in motion. Mynatt led a remarkable life: in the midst of political crises, surviving and

---

[221] *The British Book Trade: An Oral History*, p. 108.

[222] 'Margaret Mynatt', in *The Times*, 28 February 1977, p. 14.

[223] Yvonne Kapp and Margaret Mynatt, *British Policy and the Refugees, 1933–41* (London: Frank Cass, 1997). The publication year was delayed because of the appearance of a very similar title, LaFitte's *The Internment of Aliens*, published by Penguin in 1940.

[224] Richard Dove, 'British Policy and the Refugees 1933–41'. *Journal of European Studies* 29.3, September 1999, p. 321. *Gale Academic OneFile*, link.gale.com/apps/doc/A58055941/AONE?u=ucl_ttda&sid=bookmark-AONE&xid=7ebb1477. Accessed 14 May 2024.

[225] Charmian Brinson, 'Foreword', in Kapp and Mynatt, p. xvi.

constantly finding work which kept her an active political player despite the risks, the surveillance, and the impact on her health, her bookselling career was far more (as was the work of all the other women in this Element, in some form or another) than selling books.

London General and Academic Booksellers: Elizabeth Weiler, Gerti Kvergic, Christina Foyle, Una Dillon
Elizabeth Weiler

Elizabeth Weiler ran the Chelsea Bookshop on the King's Road, which she began in 1947. After going to Cambridge and studying for a history degree in 1924, she went on to do a social science diploma at the LSE in 1925, after which she became a millinery buyer for a department store in Liverpool. This was not a role she was good at, so in 1933 she joined forces with a friend to open the Norbury Bookshop but in 1939 decided she needed to be part of the war effort, so went to work in the admin office of a munitions factory. A short period post-war of working for John Lewis followed, after which the Chelsea Bookshop was started.

'She was', said Trevor Moore, a publisher's rep, 'a formidable figure – a large lady with a deep voice and grey hair tied back in a bun. But great fun to deal with – always interested and positive and chatty.'[226] Ian Norrie judged her 'an intelligent, intellectual woman. She understood the Chelsea public and was an excellent bookseller'.[227] A profile piece in *Bookselling News* warned 'she can be formidable when roused'.[228] Maureen Condon, another bookseller, picked up this use of 'formidable' and remarked, 'That woman had real cause to be "formidable"; but you never heard people say that about their male equivalents in the trade. You heard, "he's a remarkably intelligent person; he knows the trade backwards and he's a fantastic bookseller."'[229]

Miss Weiler was, then, celebrated for her bookselling skills: in 1972 she was acknowledged by the London Branch of the Booksellers Association as

---

[226] Trevor Moore, *The British Book Trade: An Oral History*, p. 107.

[227] Ian Norrie, *The British Book Trade: An Oral History*, p. 107.

[228] 'Profile: Miss Elizabeth Weiler', *Bookselling News*, May 1970, p. 40.

[229] Maureen Condon, *The British Book Trade: An Oral History*, p. 108.

having given 'unstinting service' to it since she joined the trade twenty-five years earlier. She was Chairman of the London Branch between 1965 and 1967, and served on the main Association's Council. She set up a committee in 1968 which looked at association membership, transforming the system so that there were no longer 'associate' members: instead everyone was a full member, just on different level of membership title, depending on their years of bookselling experience. This scheme meant, Weiler said, that 'a much more professional attitude to bookselling, on the continental pattern' would follow. She hoped 'it would make everyone in bookselling feel that he or she belonged to a worthwhile profession, and enable book-shops to benefit from the enthusiasm of their assistants'.[230] Other areas of the trade she focussed on were Education (she lectured at the Gomshall residential schools on at least two occasions, in 1957 and 1963) trade terms, and Book Tokens, and she was a strong advocate for the need for both publishers and booksellers to encourage people to see 'the ownership of a personal library as a status symbol',[231] in an age of Welfare State, public libraries and education.

When she retired in 1974, three former Bookselling Association Presidents, almost the whole of the London Branch committee, and 'a sprinkling of other "big names"' from the Branch were present: Una Dillon and Gerti Kvergic are mentioned, too, showing how wide her network and impact had been. The presentation of a coffee set and a Harrod's voucher came with a comment recalling her 'trenchant, often salty comments' at meetings, which Miss Weiler obviously took good humouredly, because her response was to emphasise how friendly bookselling was, and how many of her colleagues had grown into good friends.[232]

Elizabeth Weiler died in 1999 at the age of 96. Obituaries were short, and Ian Norrie gives her one brief mention in the fifth edition of *Publishing and*

---

[230] Elizabeth Weiler quoted in 'Individual Membership', *The Bookseller*, 11 May 1968, p. 2284.

[231] Elizabeth Weiler, quoted in 'Joint Session Discussion', *The Bookseller*, 15 June 1963, p. 2182.

[232] See Tony Hall, 'Presentation to Miss Weiler', *The Bookseller*, 30 November 1974, pp. 2759–2760.

Bookselling ('further down King's Road Elizabeth Weiler had the Chelsea Bookshop')[233] deleting even this from the sixth edition. She is undoubtedly a bookseller who deserves more attention than these afford her successful and wide-ranging career.

Gerti Kvergic

Gertrude (Gerti) Kvergic was born in 1907 in Vienna, and established a lending library and bookshop specialising in English and French literature there in 1925 with a female colleague. Freud was amongst this library's great supporters. The Nazis destroyed this shop when they entered Austria in 1938, and as a Jew, Kvergic was then at great risk: her non-Jewish husband managed to get Turkish visas for them both, and they then managed to escape to Britain, and settled in Cambridge, where Kvergic worked for Bowes & Bowes, one of the key bookshops there at the time. Unlike Margaret Mynatt, she was exempt from the mass internment of refugees in 1940. In 1944 she published an article in *The Spectator*, 'Book-Famished Europe', where she describes the 'paradise of booklovers and booksellers' which Cambridge represented, and marvels that after five years of war the bookshop shelves are still stocked with books.[234] In this powerful short article, she makes the case for sending out books to all the people affected by the War: she believed passionately in the power of books to mediate a healthy world-view. These people, she outlines, 'will need at once food and medicines and clothes; on that everybody agrees'. But, she exhorts,

> Let us add to this some books. Let the relief-trains ... include at an early stage small libraries in two or three languages, containing a few recent books on various subjects of immediate interest, and let those small libraries be the first heralds of more. Give them as a name, if name is needed, 'Peace Libraries', or 'Friendship Libraries', ... Let those libraries be an intelligence service. Nothing makes people talk more easily than books, or gives them so much

[233] *Publishing and Bookselling*, 5th Ed., p. 562.
[234] Gerti Kvergic, 'Book-Famished Europe', *The Spectator*, 26 May 1944, p. 472.

confidence. How they react to those first libraries, whether they ask for more and what they ask for, will serve as measure of their spiritual fitness or apathy.[235]

In 1947, when the London School of Economics decided to open a bookshop to serve its students and the readers of *The Economist* journal, she was chosen from among 80 candidates to manage this new book space.[236] She built a world-wide reputation for the shop, achieved through being as successful at mail-order selling as via footfall in the shop itself. The shop began life in St Clements Passage, and then moved to bigger premises in 1961, in Clare Market. Eventually the shop was bought by Waterstones, in 1992, although the name was kept. Sadly, in 2021 the decision was taken to close this branch down, so another piece of history is at risk of being obscured forever.

Kvergic's presence and skills as a bookseller were the cause of several noteworthy stories: she was most proud of persuading Sir Stanley Unwin to increase his firm's discount on her orders from 21 to 32 per cent, and, like Una Dillon, she preferred when possible to go around London and collect book orders from the various trade desks herself, 'in order to study the relative efficiency of different publishers'.[237] Like several of the other women in this Element, she used clothing props. For these particular trips, she tried to remain incognito:

> She rather naively supposed that if she called at trade counters in a black veil, no-one would know who she was: exactly the opposite was true, the mysterious veiled lady causing gossip everywhere.[238]

By all accounts, she was, without the veil, a striking figure. One contemporary described her as

[235] Ibid., p. 472.
[236] See Mervyn Horder, 'Gerti', in *The Bookseller*, 14 November 1986, p. 1954.
[237] Ibid. [238] Ibid.

Quite a tall lady . . . she always wore shoes with a good two inches of heel. Dark hair, and dark eyes that were made very big by thick glasses. She wore orangey-red lipstick and nice clothes – brown or grey and very classy.[239]

Mervyn Horder, who wrote her obituary in *The Bookseller*, called her 'commandingly handsome, with dark sunken eyes and a superb profile',[240] and elsewhere she is labelled 'redoubtable'[241] and 'remarkable'[242] with praise for her ability to build the highly successful mail order side of the business, as well as wry reflections on her ability to intimidate sales reps: 'the men used to say, "that woman scares me stiff"'[243], and in a longer anecdote, Cherry Lewis describes how:

When the travellers called . . . they would whisper 'is Mrs K in?' . . . There was one rep who would always say 'I am allergic to Gerti Kvergic.' He always said it, and we always laughed. The travellers treated her as a joke. Mrs Kvergic *wasn't* a joke; she was a very remarkable woman. She was running a successful business . . . and she was extremely intelligent and knowledgeable about her subject.[244]

Gerti Kvergic was also described as being 'abrupt and sharp, dogmatic and impatient'[245] and a difficult person to manage at trade meetings because of her outspokenness, but her obituary in *The Times* praised her 'international orientation, rare among booksellers at the time; a fierce precision and grasp

---

[239] Comment by Cherry Lewis, in *The British Book Trade: An Oral History*, p. 123.

[240] Horder, p. 1954. Horder worked for Duckworth Books, a publisher which Kvergic became a director of between 1961 and 1968.

[241] 'Gerald Bartlett', *The Times*, 10 May 2003, p. 40.

[242] *Publishing and Bookselling*, 6th Ed., p. 207.

[243] Comment by Maureen Condon, in *The British Book Trade: An Oral History*, p. 108.

[244] *The British Book Trade: An Oral History*, p. 124.

[245] Comment by John Prime, *The British Book Trade: An Oral History*, p. 122.

of detail; a wide knowledge of the subjects and contents of the books she was selling; and an absolute refusal to accept second-best'. Her toughness, the piece goes on, 'while quite genuine, was combined with charm, and masked warmth and humour towards those she liked and respected'.[246]

There is, too, ample evidence from pages of *The Bookseller*, both of Kvergic's outspokenness on issues around bookselling, and of the respect she inspired in others, and although space in this Element does not allow for a fuller analysis of this, further work will follow. She was a regular attender at both London Branch and national Booksellers Association gatherings, and the letters pages of *The Bookseller* show her voice raised regarding many different concerns. Pieces such as 'How to Prevent the Sale of Books' illustrate how stinging she could be towards publishers. This article explains why the policy of some publishers to charge more for orders of a single title in low numbers, or not to combine low number orders for different titles into one consignment, is a counterproductive move for more book sales (particularly for academic texts): 'in short, the attitude of some publishers defies the principle of regular stock control'.[247]

In 1971 she wrote a piece for *Bookselling News*, 'Thoughts on the Psychology of Bookselling', in which she sets out her beliefs about how to be a successful bookseller: 'it is not only your balance sheet which must balance; your judgement must as well and for that you must cultivate the three functions: imagination, intuition, and plain common sense'.[248]

For now, let this praise, from a keynote speech at the 1959 Booksellers Association Conference in Scarborough, by A. T. G. Pocock, then sales manager of Oxford University Press, signpost just how significant she was:

> Mrs Kvergic of the Economist Bookshop seems to me to fill the functions of a specialist shop in the most lively, intelligent, and forceful way imaginable. Our confidence not only

[246] 'Mrs Gerti Kvergic', *The Times*, 14 November 1986, p. 22.

[247] Gerti Kvergic, 'How to Prevent the Sale of Books', *The Bookseller*, 9 September 1967, p. 1648.

[248] Gerti Kvergic, 'Thoughts on the Psychology of Bookselling', *Bookselling News*, May/June 1971, p. 15.

in her grasp and judgement of the market but of her ency-
clopaedic knowledge of practically all that has been published
in that field of learning means that we can gauge to a nicety
whatever publicity we undertake for her. Most important, her
reasoned and astute criticism of our own shortcomings seem
to me to lead to exactly that kind of bookseller-publisher co-
operation that we must all strive for.[249]

Clearly not all sales staff from publishers felt she was a joke. And indeed, so
keen was Horder to emphasise her more approachable side, that he wrote
into *The Bookseller* to ask that a paragraph which had been cut from his
obituary be given the space via his letter. It said:

She enjoyed cooking Viennese meals for her lucky friends,
was knowledgeable on psychology, and a regular attender at
Jungian gatherings in London, and had an unexpected
fondness for birds and dogs.[250]

He ends, 'without this sentence, readers who never knew her may have
thought her a more formidable lady than she ever was'.[251]

Christina Foyle

Perhaps the female London bookseller most familiar to people is Christina
Foyle. She took over the family business in 1963, but had been working in the
bookshop since 1928. When Foyles moved to 119 Charing Cross Road in 1929,
it had an estimated 30 miles of shelving: chaotic in organisation, but the biggest
bookshop in existence for some decades. In 1930, after Christina launched her
literary lunches, holding ten every year, she became a fixture of the London
literary scene. These events often drew more than a thousand paying guests,
and were covered in the press of the time, which made Christina somewhat of

---

[249] A. T. G. Pocock, 'How the Bookseller Can Help the Publisher Sell More
Books', *The Bookseller*, 6 June 1959, p. 1944.

[250] Letter from Mervyn Horder, *The Bookseller*, 28 November 1986, p. 2157.

[251] Ibid.

Figure 2 A cigarette card showing Christina Foyle

a celebrity – so much so that she was chosen to appear on a set of cigarette cards (see Figure 2).

Her hobbies are listed as 'yachting, reading and skating'. As a celebrity, the rhetoric around her is very different to that already examined: clearly she was very far from fitting the 'ravelled cardigan' image of a bookseller seen earlier. In an article written about her for the popular magazine, *The Sketch*, in 1956, she is described like this:

There's nothing of the bookworm or bluestocking about Christina Foyle ... My first impression was of a study in grey – grey eyes, grey hair, grey suit, muted and blended in tone like a good pencil drawing.

In the article Christina talks about the importance of remaining womanly within the business world, saying that men did not like it when women tried to copy them. Clothes, she claims, are part of her armoury: 'I think clothes and appearance matter very much for the woman in business'.[252] An earlier article, in *The Bystander* in 1937, details how she had increased the turnover of Foyles from £400,000 to over a million at the age of 26 through running different book clubs and a lending library, and, of course, the luncheons. 'And yet', the article goes on, 'when you meet her, you find a shy-looking girl with a pink ribbon in her dark hair, with a soft voice, and a habit of turning and dropping her head as she talks and plays methodically with the pencils in her small white hands . . . Christina Foyle likes cheese and claret and Capri and swimming and getting her own way'.[253]

Several pieces written about her emphasise her voice – not as 'soft', as it is described above, but as 'high-pitched . . . [like] someone who had just inhaled helium'.[254] She had a 'high-pitched, rather reedy voice that often drawled away into a register too low to be heard',[255] or as a 'genteel little-girl tone of voice'.[256] Later interviews and reports make much of her regal image, and nicknames such as the Red Queen of Charing Cross Road, and The Iron Lady of the Book Trade, underline a reputation for autocratic management and idiosyncratic working practices. But, despite claims

[252] Judy Fallon, 'Books? I've Always Loved Them', *The Sketch*, 23 May 1956, p. 340.

[253] Charles Graves, 'More Celebrities in Cameo: Miss Christina Foyle', *The Bystander*, 24 November 1937, p. 281.

[254] Warren Hodge, 'Christina Foyle, 88, the Queen Of the London Bookstore, Dies' *New York Times*, 11 June 1999, p. A31

[255] Ian Norrie, 'Obituary: Christina Foyle', *The Independent*, 11 June 1999, p. 6.

[256] Dennis Barker, 'Obituary: Christina Foyle: The Power behind the Biggest Bookshop in the World, as Well as a Legendary Series of Literary Lunches', *The Guardian*, 10 June 1999, p. 22.

that she treated her staff badly, and resisted any attempts at modernising the shop or its systems, it must be remembered that, as one obituary emphasised:

> She proved that a successful large bookshop – incorporating book clubs, a lecture agency, an art gallery, two publishing imprints and the longest running series of literary luncheons ever – could be managed by a woman, at a time when the founders of Virago were still in nappies. She was also, probably, the first English bookseller, not primarily antiquarian, to become a millionaire.[257]

There is no doubt she knew about bookselling; in an article she wrote for the *Journal of the Royal Society of Arts* in 1953, she speaks authoritatively about what sells and the challenges of facing 'the great flood of new books' and choosing which to stock. She sums up the attraction of bookselling as a career by remarking that 'there is an endless fascination in bookselling, even more than in publishing, because for a publisher there are two entirely different kinds of books, his own and other publishers, whereas the bookseller can be all things to all books'.[258]

A proper biography of Christina Foyle is overdue, and her place in book trade history – and in establishing and fostering aspects of literary culture during her lifetime, – needs to be properly acknowledged. Like all the women mentioned in this Element, she had spirit and was not afraid to speak her mind. One story about her was that on hearing that Hitler was burning books in Germany, she wrote to him to ask that he send them to her instead, horrified that they were being destroyed. Apparently he replied to say he would not want the books to corrupt English readers any more than he wanted them to corrupt German ones. It is said (although sadly not proved)

---

[257] Ian Norrie, 'The Iron Lady of the Book Trade', *The Bookseller*, 18 July 1999, p. 12.

[258] Christina Foyle, 'The Bookseller and the Reading Public', *Journal of the Royal Society of Arts*, 18 September 1953, p. 779.

that Christina took her revenge by lining the rooftop of the bookshop with copies of *Mein Kampf* to protect it from wartime bombings.[259]

Christina Foyle had considerable skill as a publicist, and according to Ian Norrie, she 'wove fantasies' which were then reported in the press interviews she gave fairly frequently, positioning Foyles as a charitable concern, more of a library than a bookshop, run by the family for the benefit of the nation. She was not active in the Booksellers Association, or branch activities, and was not a supporter of the Net Book Agreement. Evidence from *The Bookseller* is sparse; she clearly kept herself apart from industry gatherings, 'buttressed by absolute power and her considerable fortune',[260] and in an insightful interview she reveals her aversion to any kind of organised management structure, which may explain why she was never interested in collaborating with other bookselling colleagues:

> We like the whole place to be a bookshop, so we don't have personnel departments, we don't file anything. We've never had a board meeting in history . . . Ronald and I run it really like a fairground: no-one else would do it the same way, they'd think we were crazy.[261]

She enjoyed living at Beeleigh, the medieval abbey in Essex her father had bought, installing in it what is reported to have been a spectacular book collection. In later life she lived here with cats, tortoises and peacocks, but she was still commuting back to London after the weekend until she was well into her 80s. She was a controversial figure in the book trade, but has

---

[259] These incidents are, however, unreliably claimed as having Christina, rather than her father William, as the main character. For example, in Penny Mountain 's *Foyles: A Celebration* (London: Foyles, 2003) the attempt to get Hitler to send books to Foyles is accredited to William (p. 71); in an article in *The Guardian*, this is attributed to Christina (Martin Wainwright, 'Shelling out for Foyles Pets', *The Guardian*, 8 December 1999, p. 2).

[260] Hodge, p. A31.

[261] Christina Foyle quoted in Susan Raven, 'A day in the life of Christina Foyle', *The Bookseller*, 22 May 1982, p. 1957.

left behind a bookshop whose iconic status means it is still known as Foyles, despite now also being owned by Waterstones.

Una J. Dillon

In contrast, there is Una Dillon, who a *Guardian* reporter, in 1986, called the 'unknown doyenne of London booksellers'. The piece goes on: 'discreet, demure, non-aggressive and publicity shy, she is the opposite of her sister-in-trade, Christina Foyle'.[262] In many ways the literal 'foil' to her more widely known counterpart, Una Dillon would build what turned out to be another iconic London bookshop in Bloomsbury.

Agnes Joseph Madeline Dillon (known as Una) was born on the 8 January 1903 in Cricklewood, London. She was the fifth of six children; her father was a train engineer, later company secretary, and her mother was a teacher, and both were Catholic. They insisted all their children received a good education. There were four daughters: one went on to become a nun, and the other three remained in London, living together for much of their adult lives, and all having notable careers. Tess became one of the first female Heads of Physics, at Queen Elizabeth College (which merged with King's College, London in 1985), and counted among her friends Margaret, 2nd Viscountess of Rhondda, who began and ran the influential Bloomsbury-based journal, *Time and Tide*; Carmen was an Oscar-award-winning film art director who worked on productions such as Laurence Olivier's *Hamlet*, and other iconic films such as *The Prince and the Showgirl*, *To Catch a Thief*, and *The Go-Between*. After following her sister Tess to complete a physics degree at Bedford College, Una realised that she had little interest in an academic career, and found a job working for the Central Association for Mental Welfare (now MIND). This experience, which involved supplying books for special courses for medical officers of health and teachers of children with special needs introduced her to 'what seemed an attractive world peopled by those who were helpful and dedicated to the spread of books'.[263]

---

[262] John Cunningham, 'Denials of the Misses Dillon', *The Guardian*, 16 July 1986, p. 10.

[263] Una Dillon, 'Looking Back and Forward', *The Bookseller*, 16 September 1967, p. 1714.

It is tempting to skip over this period of Dillon's history, but it is worth underlining that she worked in this role for over a decade, a considerable time which built up her contacts in the book trade, and her understanding about how it operated. When she says, then, that she 'came to the trade in complete ignorance and ... innocence of the pitfalls of business life' and 'looking back I was almost irresponsible in setting out to start a bookshop with a total capital of £800 and little knowledge',[264] it is to modestly undersell what skills she did bring when, in 1936, she took over a small library supplier's business at 9 Store Street, London. With a loan from her father of £600, and £200 more from a friend, Una Dillon began her own bookshop, a leap of entrepreneurial confidence which was to be proved more than a naïve risk: as her *Dictionary of National Biography* entry evocatively details, she quickly became known as a 'formidable business-woman' and 'a familiar sight flying around London on an old bicycle – a tweed-suited Valkyrie determined to fill a customer's order within eight hours'.[265] She took advantage of what she calls the 'halcyon days' of the book trade of the time, when there were far less books published, and when publishers were generous with terms, and books could be obtained swiftly from the wholesalers, Simpkin Marshall, who were not far away, on Paternoster Row. These facts should not detract from a recognition of Miss Dillon's business shrewdness, however. She had picked her venue strategically, as she reveals:

> Personal contacts with university staff, in particular through my sister, then head of the physics department of one of the colleges, brought the first customers and together with literary minded residents of Bloomsbury (a larger population than now exists) the shop began to be reasonably busy and slowly to pay its way.[266]

[264] Ibid., p. 1714.
[265] Jean H. Cook, 'Dillon, Agnes Joseph Madeline [Una]', in the *Oxford Dictionary of National Biography*.
[266] Ibid.

Bookselling is a demanding job, as the preceding parts of this Element have detailed; the 1930s were not the easiest of times during which to begin a new bookshop. Yet Una Dillon, by all accounts, started from scratch, and by the time the Second World War began three years later, had established a viable and even flourishing, business.

London around Bloomsbury in 1936 was a hub of activity, particularly for the book trade. Close by, the Woolfs lived in Tavistock Square, and T. S. Eliot was working at Faber & Faber in Russell Square. The British Museum with its famous Round Reading Room was there, too, in Great Russell Street, and not very far away, most of the major publishing houses were based around Paternoster Row, as was Simpkin Marshall, the dominant book wholesaling firm. Penguin paperbacks were still just newcomers to the book world, having launched the year before. Foyles, on Charing Cross Road, was not only the largest bookshop in the capital, but also the most innovative: Christina Foyle's literary luncheons in 1936 included Dorothy L. Sayers, Sylvia Pankhurst, the Emperor of Ethiopia, and Peggy Ashcroft as speakers. The area around Store Street and Malet Place and Gower Street would have looked very different: Senate House was not yet finished, and many of University College London's current buildings were not in existence. Foster Court had only just been turned from a department store's warehouse and stables into the Department for Zoology and Comparative Anatomy; and the distinctive Flemish Franco-Gothic building, built by Charles Fitzroy Doll, which is now Waterstones Gower Street, was at that point a terrace of small shops with apartments over the top of them.

The year 1936 was the year of George V's death, and the accession and abdication of Edward VIII. It was the year when the Olympics were held in Berlin, Germany occupied the Rhineland, and the Spanish Civil War started. Stanley Baldwin had become the British Prime Minister the year before, Turing introduced the idea of the Turing machine to the London Mathematical Society, and the miners marched from Jarrow to London.

So, the contexts within which Una Dillon starts her bookselling career are both auspicious and foreboding; she is able to capitalise on the intellectual institutions situated very close to her shop, the student population, and her own contacts with academics; her own existing connections with publishers, too, helped her in obtaining a regular and varied supply of stock, but there were a scant three years of trading before the Second World War broke out, and significant new challenges loomed.

When the Second World War began, the area of London around Una Dillon's bookshop changed dramatically; the university colleges evacuated their departments to other universities in less at-risk areas of the UK, and Senate House was taken over by the Ministry of Information. In an article written in 1967, the year of her retirement, Una, in typically unfussy manner, describes her response: 'It was a case then of the mountain going to Mohammed and in the autumn I was off with packing cases of books to Cardiff, to Leicester and to Knebworth House where Froebel Training College had moved.'[267] As Peter Stockham, her successor as manager of the University Bookshop said, 'she found in this positive service a similar cause to that which she had found in her earlier charitable work'.[268] The commitment to her customers kept her in London throughout the War, working under extremely challenging conditions. Una described the 'terrible' impact on the book trade of the bombing of the City when many of the major publishing houses were hit around Paternoster Row, including Simpkin Marshall. This made distribution and access to books a challenge, but there were still some trade counters left open, and Una was there, with her 'battered bicycle', which, she says, 'became a familiar sight to many of them, and friendships made with men at trade counters were most valuable to me later on'.[269] Though the bookshop had lost a lot of its previously regular customers, it picked up new ones from the journalists and writers who worked at the MOI, and some, like John Betjeman and Cecil Day Lewis, became firm friends with Miss Dillon.

Bombs meant the shop itself had to adapt; Una described how a heavy bomb fell with tragic results on the West Central Jewish Club just behind the bookshop and the back of the shop was badly blasted and made unusable. By luck a shop on the opposite side of the road was empty (that owner, Una relates later, having run away to the country) and so she was able to buy it, and move Dillon's over with the help of friends, some of the MOI staff and the University Library trolleys[270] (see Figure 3). These details underline the

[267] Una Dillon, 'Looking back and forward', *The Bookseller*, 16 September 1967, p. 1714.
[268] Peter Stockham, 'Obituary: Una Dillon', *The Independent*, 17 April 1993, p. 15.
[269] 'Looking back and forward', p. 1715. [270] Ibid.

Figure 3 Image of Dillon Bookshop 33 Store Street

support which the shop, and its owner had, and the determination and courage it must have taken to have kept going. Today that space is still a bookshop, Treadwells, an esoteric specialist selling old and new books.[271]

Una's aim was to create a 'really good general shop with an academic slant',[272] but the size of her premises precluded much in the way of expansion. Instead, she focussed on aligning her stock carefully with local

---

[271] See www.treadwells-london.com/. Accessed 26 April 2024.
[272] 'Looking back and forward', p. 1715.

needs; for instance, after the War the Institute of Education began a teacher training course for Commonwealth students, and she catered for these new customers by laying the foundations of what she says she 'can justly claim to be one of the best departments of education and of books on Africa in the book trade' of the time.[273]

Over the next decade, the Dillon Bookshop established itself as a quietly successful part of the area. Meanwhile, post-Second World War, the colleges of London University had returned to their home sites, and a period of expansion in higher education began: between 1948 and 1957 the universities of Nottingham, Southampton, Hull, Exeter and Leicester were all established from former university colleges, and the 1960s saw a university expansion which doubled the amount of degree offering institutions in the UK. Numbers of students were rising as a consequence (although still approximately a tenth of what they are today), so discussions about expanding facilities necessarily followed. The report of the University Grants Committee on British Universities for the period 1929–1935 contained the following advice, in the section dealing with libraries:

> In some, in indeed we might say in most, of the provincial Universities, we were struck by the inadequacy of the bookshops in the vicinity of the University. In one of two cases we believe this difficulty has been met by an arrangement for supplying the necessary accommodation for a bookshop within the University precincts. Should bookshop facilities be inadequate in the case of any individual institution, it might, we suggest, be desirable for the University authorities to address a representation on the matter to such a body as the Associated Booksellers of Great Britain and Ireland; if private enterprise is for any reason unable to satisfy the requirements of the situation, some alternative arrangement to meet a real need may have to be devised.[274]

---

[273] Ibid.

[274] University Grants Committee on British Universities, 1929–1935, quoted in documents relating to the need for a university bookshop in Senate House Special Collections, File MS926/2.

By 1950, within the University of London, there were moves afoot to provide its staff and students with something which would do for it what Heffer's and Blackwell's were doing for Cambridge and Oxford Universities. The initiative was helped by the proactive support given by four men: William Hogarth, Clerk of the University Court from 1948 to 1950 and then the first Secretary of the Athlone Press (the first University of London publishing venture); Professor Hugh Bellot, Chair of the Athlone Press Board, who became Vice-Chancellor of the University in 1951; Dr Douglas Logan, who was Clerk of the Court of London University from 1944, becoming the Principal in 1948; and Lord William Piercy, Chairman of the Industrial and Commercial Finance Corporation. Hogarth had sent a memo to Logan in 1950, stressing the need for a bookshop – suggesting the establishment of a first-class bookshop in two or three of the Torrington place shops.[275] At the time the University of London was still negotiating terms for these buildings with the Bedford Estate, and there was the added complication, even when ownership was transferred, that the buildings were full of what Logan called 'a motley lot plying trades inappropriate to a University Precinct'[276] (see Figure 4).

He had also taken this call to Professor Bellot, who was a great supporter of access to books: Bellot believed 'books were not to be hidden in glass cases

---

[275] See draft chapter for a proposed book about Dillons, p. 4 (which sadly never seems to have been completed). by Douglas Logan, in Senate House Special Collections, File MS926/2. One of the most tantalising threads I uncovered whilst doing this research was finding correspondence (and I think, some of the draft chapters) for a proposed history of Dillons: Some of this is in Senate House Library Special Collections, some in the LSE Special Collections: dated 1979, there are letters from Grant Paton, then Managing Director of Dillons, to Sir Douglas Logan, asking if he would be willing to contribute a chapter. There is an outline proposal for the book, and then the draft chapter from Sir Douglas, but no indication of whether this was sent off, or the book went any further. The LSE archive holds what I think is Peter Stockham's draft chapter, and part of one other, but with no surrounding correspondence. It was only because I had first visited Senate House library that I connected these documents together – illustrating what can sometimes feel like miraculous finds, but also underlining the knife edge research rests upon when working in these areas.

[276] Ibid., p. 4.

Figure 4 Image of Torrington Place Shops, year unknown

or kept in stacks difficult to access. So far as possible they should be kept on open shelves, where the sight of them and the temptation to browse among them were part of an undergraduate's education, science students as much as art students'.[277] Bellot's special interest in university bookshops came from having been impressed by the contributions they had made to campuses, particularly in Nigeria. While he accepted the fact that plans would have to wait for the premises to become available in 1954, he outlined his ideas to one of the most respected booksellers of the time, Hubert Wilson, who he had been at school with. Wilson was encouraging, and so Bellot instructed Logan to put together an estimate of the costs involved. Logan also had help from Wilson – and from another great female bookseller of the period, Gerti Kvergic, who, as the brief outline of her life and work in the earlier section

[277] From draft notes for the proposed book on Dillons, I believe by Professor R. A. Humphreys, in Senate House Special Collections, File MS926/ 2.

shows, was well-placed and well-respected as a bookseller to give advice regarding the London University Bookshop project.

By 1954, therefore, the situation regarding the proposed bookshop had moved forward considerably. Some of the Torrington Place shops were going to become vacant, and the plans Bellot had put together had had positive responses from other booksellers. A University Bookshop Committee was set up to take action, and negotiations began to find a partner bookseller to launch the new shop.

Una Dillon's shop was one of a handful which already served the University of London in the Bloomsbury area. The main others, slightly closer, were a specialist medical bookshop, H. K. Lewis, whose sign can still be seen high up on the wall of the building near the entrance to Euston Square tube station, now a UCL coffee shop, and the International University Booksellers Ltd, which occupied parts of two buildings owned by the University at the other end of Gower Street, at numbers 92 and 94. The Committee first considered a partnership with International University Booksellers, but discovered that they were not financially stable, so H. K. Lewis & Co. Ltd was brought into discussions. When, this, too, fell through, and there was no interest from Blackwell's or from Bryce's Bookshop, in Museum Street, they approached Una Dillon. She was ready. Logan prepared her case with the Committee, saying:

> Her turnover at present is about £8000 a year. It therefore follows that she could start out only on a modest scale compared with the other firms which have been approached. On the other hand, she is eager to take the opportunity and I feel that, in many ways, she has a better understanding of the type of bookshop which the Court have in mind than any of the other people with whom the project has been discussed. It is not perhaps irrelevant that Miss Dillon is a graduate of the University and that her sister is on the staff of Queen Elizabeth College so that is fairly well known in University circles.[278]

[278] See Dr Douglas Logan, address to the Court of London University, dated 4 July 1955, in Senate House Special Collections, File MS926/2.

The same meeting then considered the plans Una had submitted: in a succinct but comprehensive document, Miss Dillon sets out how she wants to set up the bookshop, and what she believes will bring in a strong turnover. She states her aims at the very beginning:

> The shop should be an attractive general bookshop giving efficient, quick and amiable service. The academic requirements of students, lecturers and libraries should form the foundation of the trade, but what is best of modern literature, books on Art, Drama, Travel, etc., should be displayed as an inducement to students to use the shop liberally for their leisure and for the widening of their interests outside the confines of their own subjects. I think I can say that I already have in Store Street the goodwill of many lecturers and University staff who come to my shop for books outside their professional needs.[279]

This confidence was not unfounded, but despite the advocacy of Logan, Peter Stockham, who had joined the Store Street shop staff just before the move to Malet Street in 1956, remembers that:

> many people in the trade felt that no large bookshop could prosper in such an isolated setting away from the West End. They were wrong. By attempting a high level of personal service and stressing the ability to care, the bookshop grew.[280]

In a letter written to Logan in July 1955, Una Dillon makes this assertion: 'I know', she said, 'that you are gambling on my capability to carry it through and I shall do all I can to come up to your expectations.'[281]

[279] See Una Dillon, 'Preliminary Proposals for the Creation of a University Bookshop at Malet Street, WC1', in Senate House Special Collections, File MS926/8/2.

[280] 'Obituary: Una Dillon', *The Independent*, 17 April 1993, p. 15.

[281] Letter from Una Dillon to Dr Douglas Logan, 20 July 1955. In Senate House Library Special Collections, file MS926/8/2.

The Dillons University Bookshop company was set up in 1956, with the Directors being Lord Piercy, Mr Hogarth, Douglas Logan and Miss Dillon. Una had negotiated the value of her Store Street stock, to be transferred into shares in the company, a salary of £900 per annum, and that she be appointed as Managing Director for the next eight years. The sums involved were realistic, and she got everything she asked for. In the end, she was to stay on for eleven years, having to shelve plans for early retirement, because the business was continuing to grow successfully. Her work ethic is clear in this business plan – she sets out how she will attract students towards more general trade books, listing ambitions to stock Pans and Penguins, Fontana paperbacks, World's Classics, Everyman books, and maps and guides. Evening openings to accommodate Birkbeck students, and a portable bookstall to take to University events, would be included. In short, she says, 'I should be willing to take a great deal of trouble, possibly for a small initial return in sales, to attract students and their friends to the shop, and I would willingly give freely of my spare time to this end.'[282]

The new bookshop opened to the public on Monday the 10th September 1956. To begin with it occupied just the corner of Malet Street, in the two vacated shop spaces of numbers 54 and 56 Torrington Place. Over the next few years the shop expanded as the other properties became vacant, so that it eventually occupied most of the block taken up by Waterstones Gower Street today, as seen in Figure 5.

Una Dillon's creative flair was evident in the design of the interior of the shop: this article from a 1962 edition of *British Books* gives us this evocative description:

> It is a shop full of young people, made for young people – the young people who live in Bloomsbury, many of them students at London University. Situated on a corner site in Bloomsbury, only a few hundred yards from the University Senate House and opposite the Students' Union, it is a bright and cheerful shop, with the ground floor enjoying natural daylight from the range of full-length plate glass windows. People who like

---

[282] Dillon, 'Preliminary Proposals'.

Figure 5 A picture of Dillons University Bookshop

> a bookshop of the traditional dark and musty atmosphere would
> be horrified by Dillon's. It has lightly painted walls and beauti-
> ful, soft-coloured Lundia wood shelving. Contemporary light
> fittings and elegant modern staircases complete the picture of
> a colourful fresh place in which to peruse books quietly and at
> leisure.[283]

The Lundia shelving mentioned here was produced exclusively in Britain
by an organisation called Remploy, established after the 1944 Disabled
Persons (Employment) Act to directly employ disabled people in specialist
factories. One of these dealt in shop fittings – and was used to install the
Lundia shelving in polished African Abura hardwood throughout the
shop. The Lundia system was designed so that it could be continually
added to from the range – at the time, a development noticeable enough
to get this coverage in *British Books*. Una Dillon understood the importance

---

[283] 'Building a Growing Bookshop', *British Books*, September 1962. (Reprint found
in LSE Special Collections, file PIERCY /13/ 43). Attempts to find the original
source have so far failed.

of creating an appealing space (no doubt also picking up some ideas and advice from Carmen's experience with film sets) and she employed professional help, at considerable cost, to get this right. In a letter justifying this cost to Lord Piercy, R. G. Hutchings stresses the fact that the personal attention of the designer, Mr Timothy, 'is responsible for the whole attractive appearance of the Bookshop on which so many favourable comments have been made'.[284] The bill was paid without any argument.

Further evidence of Dillon's attention to shop fittings comes in a contribution to a pamphlet on bookshop equipment and design, where she talks knowledgeably about different kinds of floor coverings (linoleum, thermoplastic tiles, vinyl, wood, cork and cork tiles, terrazzo, and carpeting). She notes that 'three separate periods of expansion which necessitated the knitting together of four separate houses have given an opportunity for Dillons to buy different types of flooring material . . . so far, Cork-O-Plast seems to give the most satisfactory answer, though there has not been time to test its durability fully'.[285]

The contrast with Foyles, the other main London bookshop to be able to claim a large footprint, and Christina Foyle's approach, is obvious from descriptions such as this one: 'shoppers had to negotiate a bizarre docket system, which meant queuing more than once for a single purchase. The store, with its miles of shabby shelving, single tiny lift and antiquated escalator, began to look sad, unloved, and impossibly outdated'.[286]

As well as creating a bright, modern space, Una Dillon created a workplace where the well-being of her staff was of great importance. As Frances Collingwood, in a *Books* article explains:

> Apart from the obvious attractions of wide-open window-space . . ., modern décor, and enlightened display methods, there is the personality of Miss Dillon herself. I was made

---

[284] Letter from R. G. Hutchings to Lord Piercy, 22 February 1957, in LSE Special Collections, file PIERCY /13/42.

[285] Una Dillon, 'Floor Coverings for Bookshops', in *Bookshop Equipment and Design* (London: Hutchinson, 1968), p. 22.

[286] Jessica Davies, 'The Chaos Christina Left behind', *The Times*, 31 July 2001, p. 4.

conscious not only of her extreme capability as managing
director of this vast business, but also her relationship with her
staff of forty-eight men and women. A former Bumpus colleague, now working in Dillon's foreign department, told me that
such is the affection and loyalty they all feel for her that when
she is absent for any reason they all work that much harder to
make up.[287]

A former employee of Dillons also recalls Una's enlightened approach to
women: Gillian Shears, who became the manager of the African Department,
remembers when she got married being called in to see Una, who gave her
a raise, saying as they did this for male staff, she could see no reason why it
should not be done for women, too.[288] There is plenty of evidence from the
files held in Senate House Library that Una was constantly making sure her
staff were looked after – whether that was by arranging for Christmas
bonuses, or setting up a company pension scheme for them.[289]

Her long-time colleague, Peter Stockham, said that 'Dillon had great
powers of organisation and the capacity to inspire and encourage enthusiasm in others. Her selling philosophy was based on the importance of
personal service.'[290] Such was the affection with which she was held by
those she worked with that when, in July 1962, she slipped and damaged her
femur, resulting in a stay at University College Hospital, Douglas Logan
and Lord Piercy arranged for her to be transferred to a private wing. The
correspondence which survives shows real concern for her comfort and
recovery; she was clearly a valued part of University life.[291]

[287] Frances Collingwood, 'Thus Speaks the Modern Bookseller', *Books: Journal of the National Book League*, 1963, p. 190.

[288] Memory reported by Michael Seviour in *The British Book Trade: An Oral History*, p. 118.

[289] See Senate House Library Special Collections, files MS926/2, MS926/2/4, and MS926/8/2.

[290] Stockham, 'Una Dillon', *The Times*, 20 April 1993, p. 21.

[291] See letters between Douglas Logan and Lord Piercy, 16, 19, and 20 July, in LSE Special Collections, File PIERCY 13/43.

It was during this time, too, that Miss Dillon began to take an active part in the wider work of the bookselling profession, via her participation in Booksellers' Association events, and London Branch ones, too. She was a regular attender at meetings, and a committee member, and most significantly, was a founder member of the Booksellers Association's Charter Scheme, which was started in 1964 as a way to try and establish some formal standards for bookshops, with benefits if they attained Charter status which included special publisher discounts. She was constantly working to roll out good practice, and encourage greater professionalisation of bookselling – something which contributed to her CBE for services to the book trade, which was awarded to her in 1967.

Una Dillon sets out the context for university bookselling in an academic journal article published in 1964, stressing the need for effective stock:

> From the beginning, the staff and students should be able to see the fringe books on their subjects, not only new publications but the best books of past years. The university bookshop must be a general bookshop too, in the sense that there must be space allotted to a large range of paperbacks – the more lighthearted as well as the 'egg-head' – to books on art, books of general cultural interest, new poetry, and student magazines, etc. These are of great importance, for the shop should be an attraction not only for the university population but also for the general public.[292]

There are echoes here of the plans she set out in 1955, quoted from above – but now these are expanded after nine years of experience, and the confident authority now present shows. The article finishes with these optimistic hopes for the future:

> There is no doubt that university bookselling is in a period of great expansion, and with the growth of higher education the

[292] Una Dillon, 'The New Look in University Bookselling', *Journal of Documentation* 20.4, 1964, p. 198.

general bookseller can also look forward to a bright future. The children of the present generation of those receiving a higher education will surely be more book-minded and better informed at a young age than were their parents.[293]

She was also to prove an exceptionally shrewd business-woman. Douglas Logan was able to report to the University Council, in 1959, that 'the progress achieved by the bookshop over the past three years has exceeded the expectations of all those connected with it. The turnover in the first year amounted to £27430 and this rose to £45657 in the second year end and to £64095 in the third year which ended on 31 August 1959'.[294] This is quite an accomplishment when compared to the £8000 a year turnover she was making in Store Street.

The bookshop played host to many book launches and exhibitions of new books – as well as more social parties held there to showcase new expansions and anniversaries. The full guest list for an exhibition of scientific books in 1958 still exists, in the LSE Special Collections archive, and shows a wide mix of different academics, including Tess Dillon, as well as librarians and medical specialists. Later there would be royal visits – the Queen Mother visited in November 1961, sending a letter afterwards via an Equerry to say she had been 'particularly impressed by the tremendous variety of books which were displayed in such a realistic and imaginative way'.[295]

The bookshop expanded, taking over the shop space at Queen Mary College in 1966, and later others at Wye College, in Kent, and on the University campuses at Nottingham and Canterbury. By the time of Una Dillon's retirement in 1967, the company employed 109 people and was turning over £600 k a year. A retirement luncheon at the Connaught Rooms in London was held for her in September 1967, and over 150 people attended. Ivan Chambers of Bryce's Bookshop, which was in Museum Street, just round the

---

[293] Ibid., p. 202.

[294] Douglas Logan, 'Note by the Principal', 1959 in Senate House Special Collections, File MS926/2.

[295] Letter from Alastair Aird, Equerry to Queen Elizabeth the Queen Mother, to Lord Piercy, 17 November 1961, in LSE Special Collections file PIERCY 13/43.

corner from Una Dillon's first shop in Store Street, gave an address in which he praised her achievements:

> He felt sure that he had with him all the booksellers in the land, when he said that far from stealing trade from them, Miss Dillon had, in fact, so improved the image of the bookseller that they all benefitted. 'The rest of us do not envy her', he said. 'We feel that she has done *us* a service in giving booksellers a new dimension.'[296]

Even after she retired, Una continued to be connected to the book trade: she remained on the Board of Dillon's until it was sold to Pentos in 1977, continued to campaign for the Net Book Agreement to stay in place, and helped the British Council with a low-priced book scheme for overseas books. As well as her CBE, she was awarded honorary degrees by the University of London and the Open University, and was honoured at events celebrating 50 years of her being in the business in 1986, which coincided with the relaunch of Dillons,[297] under Pentos, with a massive new refurbishment, opened by Princess Anne. In an interview she gave to *Publishing News* after this event, Una (with input from Carmen) gives her judgement on the new Dillons logo – or 'looogo' as she called it (she hated it) and also the change to calling it a book *store*, rather than a book*shop* – ('it's horrible'). And she was uncomfortable about the new publicity campaign, (see Figure 6) which took a dig at Foyles, although her comments end with what is surely a roast of her own:

> I wish they would stop digging at Foyles. I know Christina Foyle is very stately and Queen Victoria, but I've always liked her myself . . . and her shop has such a lot of books. Everything, really, if you know where to find it.[298]

---

[296] 'Farewell Luncheon for Miss Dillon', *The Bookseller*, 16 September 1967, p. 1698.

[297] Apostrophe was dropped when Pentos took over the firm.

[298] Una Dillon, quoted in Fred Newman, 'Dillons Special Report: 50th Anniversary Special', *Publishing News*, 10 October 1986, p. 6.

Figure 6 Foyled again advertisement

There was a plaque unveiling at this relaunch too – which I was told was found in the refurbishment which took place in 2022, but which seems to have been lost. The one which began this research, hidden behind a bookcase, was put in place in 2000, after Waterstones had taken over and the store was rebranded again. It, too, had disappeared during the 2022 refurbishment, and remained in storage during most of the time writing this Element.

In 1986, Pentos, the new owners of Dillons Bookshops, held a Literary Dinner in honour of Una. She was presented with a solid gold medallion of the Dillons' logo (which she graciously accepted, despite her dislike of the design). At the Dinner, the Publishing Association's President, Gordon Graham, recalled that Miss Dillon used to wear a monocle, 'so she could drop it when publishers revealed their discounts',[299] a quirk which reveals something of her awareness of the impact personal style could have on perceptions of her as a business woman. This was a detail also included by Peter Stockham in one of his obituaries for Miss Dillon: 'tall, thin, and energetic, she wore a monocle and must have been a striking figure'[300] (see Figure 7). Monocles were largely an accessory worn by men, and certainly not common, or even fashionable, for women to wear them during the 1930s–1960s, so Una Dillon's choice to do so shows her appreciation of the impact this would make on her business associates:

> Worn in a woman's eye, the monocle makes an unexpectedly forceful statement of transgression. For once, it isn't funny in the least. A man in a monocle is putting on airs: He wants to be taken seriously, elevated to a status that he might not hold, but that someone of his sex could. A woman in a monocle doesn't aspire to be what she isn't; rather, she takes what she shouldn't.[301]

---

[299] Harry Barr, 'What Una Dillon Didn't Tell the Princess . . .', *Publishing News*, 3 October 1986, p. 7.

[300] Peter Stockham, 'The Empire Born in an £800 Shop', *The Daily Mail*, Wed 23 April 1993, p. 31.

[301] Ibid.

Figure 7 Image of Una Dillon at a 1961 display of Nelson Books, wearing her monocle

In other words, a monocle 'was an object whose primary purpose was to manufacture identity'.[302]

When Una Dillon died at the age of 90, there was an outpouring of respect and love for her. Letters written to her sister, Carmen, now in the BFI archive, show that she was still remembered by key people and organisations with whom she had been connected. Rayner Unwin, who became one of the Directors of the Bookshop, said:

> She was a very special person, and to me represents the spirit
> of an age that alas, seems to have passed. She was so kind to

---

[302] Marius Hentea, 'Monocles on Modernity', *Modernism/Modernity* 20.2, 2013, p.214.

me, and so unassuming, but for all that a complete professional who won everyone's respect by leading from the
front ... She was a great lady, and much loved.[303]

The Booksellers Association sent this tribute: 'She will be remembered by the
book trade with great affection. The industry has lost someone very dear and
special.'[304] And the then Principal of London University, Peter Holwell, wrote:

the work she had undertaken over the years to develop the
Torrington Place Bookshop in a way that would support
teaching and research has been deeply valued by the
University, not to mention many generations of students
and their teachers.[305]

Una Dillon managed to build a business which worked not just to become
an economic success, but also to bring benefits to the University it was part
of. In an article written about campus bookselling, Harold Bohme explains
the importance of the university bookshop:

It is sometimes not appreciated that a campus bookstore has
educational obligations towards the university community,
and that these can be as important as those of an academic
department. In a society in which books have lost their central
significance, in which the reading and discussion of books no
longer is entirely fashionable, the university must instil in its
students a feeling for the importance of reading, and a delight
in the pleasures to be had from good literature ... in some
respects it can do this even more effectively than the library,
because it not only stresses the importance of books, but the

---

[303] Letter to Carmen Dillon from Rayner Unwin, 15 April 1993. BFI archive.

[304] Letter from Tim Godfray on behalf of the BA, to Carmen Dillon, 13 May 1993.
BFI Archive.

[305] Letter to Carmen Dillon from the Principal of London University, Peter
Holwell, 21 April 1993.

importance of owning books, of building a personal library, of cultivating a taste for collecting books.[306]

Una Dillon's own philosophy on what a university bookshop should be like, as has been seen, exactly fits this – where she went beyond this was to insist that the university bookshop should serve as a space to bring the general public into as well, encouraging accessible reach of academic ideas as well as non-academic ones. In this, her vision was to acknowledge the importance of that word, 'impact', that all scholars now seek to demonstrate their research has, recognising that a bookshop can be a valuable, more neutral space for people to engage with research in than a university lecture hall can be. She never stopped trying to make books accessible: a Dillons magazine article in 1986, on the occasion of Una and her sister Carmen's retirement move from London to Hove, described how she had 'continually expanded her stock to meet the demands of London's changing population throughout the war and in the social and economic upheavals of the afterwar years'.[307]

Ultimately the most effective summary of her own impact is this one, from Peter Stockham: 'She laid great stress on helping people and giving the public the best possible service. It was this ideal, embedded in Dillon's, that was Una Dillon's great contribution to bookselling.'[308]

---

[306] Harold Bohme, 'A Bookstore on the Campus', *The University as Publisher* (Toronto University Press, 1961), p. 158.

[307] *Dillons News*, 1986 (copy in BFI archives, Carmen Dillon Collection, Box 2).

[308] Peter Stockham, 'The Empire Born in an £800 shop', p. 31.

Conclusion

The value of this research is to show not just the achievements of these women booksellers, but also how vital these bookshops were to the spread of new ideas, for getting reading material more readily into the hands of the reader, whether they sought radical, academic or general books. Bookselling is the link between the publisher and the reader, and therefore also the link between the author and the reader. Bookshops can take the virtual shape of the behemoth online retailer Amazon, or be the metaphorical 'lantern-bearers of civilisation' of Philip Pullman.[309] They can be physical spaces with iconic status, like Foyles, or smaller, but transformative locations like the Chelsea Bookshop.

Whatever shape they take, they need booksellers to manage the stock, interact with customers, and ensure the bookshop is accessible to those who visit it. Booksellers are 'cultural agents' providing the public with 'unbiased, reliable and informed personal advice'[310] but they are also part of a retail establishment where the job is primarily to sell as many books as possible. The bookshop assistant must never lose sight of that fact; bookselling is a highly specialised trade and to be a successful bookseller calls for 'knowledge and intelligence as well as a wide interest in people and an enquiring mind'.[311] Irene Babbidge's advice, published in her handbook of bookshop practice in 1965, is echoed by James Daunt, managing director of the UK's most dominant bookshop chain, Waterstones, whose three cardinal rules for successful bookselling include having friendly and informative staff,[312] and who has said that he believes 'booksellers are vocational … they care about books and about literature and they

---

[309] P. Pullman, 'Bookselling in the UK', 1 August 2017. See www.philip-pullman .com/newsitem?newsItemID=26. Accessed 10 July 2019.

[310] *Bookshops in the Cultural life of the Nation*, Booksellers Association. See www .booksellers.org.uk/BookSellers/BizFormFiles/da65dd35-ab98-44b6-b433- 2ef12bafb293.pdf. Accessed 10 July 2019.

[311] Irene Babbidge, *Beginning in Bookselling* (Andre Deutsch, 1965), p. 9.

[312] James Daunt, quoted in Ed Smith, 'A Man with Plenty of Shelf Esteem', *The Times*, 31 May 2011, p. 6[S]. The Times Digital Archive, http://tinyurl .galegroup.com/tinyurl/BL8ks1. Accessed 12 July 2019.

want to serve and help people'.[313] Babbidge's statement holds true over fifty years later because, despite the arrival of the internet and online bookselling, or perhaps because of it, there is more of a need than ever for specialists who can help the reader navigate through the vast numbers of books available to them. As Ryan Raffaelli explains:

> indie booksellers have mastered the art of 'handselling' books that are uniquely tailored to specific tastes of the readers who most frequent their stores … To accomplish this task, independent bookstores employ talent who are themselves voracious readers and possess deep knowledge and passion for books. Consequently, booksellers serve the role of matchmaker between a customer and each book on the shelves in the store … Artificial intelligence-based algorithms have yet to fully replicate the human experience associated with the art of handselling that successful independent booksellers have mastered.[314]

The achievements of Una Dillon and her contemporary women booksellers bring together histories of university organisation, retailing, women and work, radical ideas, the spread of reading and book ownership, trade structures – all, of course, part of bookselling. They raise questions about how businesses keep and make accessible their records – now and in the recent past – and illustrate how challenging it is to recreate those histories, even when relatively little time has passed since those events happened.

---

[313] James Daunt, quoted in James Dean, 'You Don't Have to Do Everything by the Book to Rescue Barnes & Noble', *The Times*, 9 November 2019, p. 55. *The Times Digital Archive*, link-gale-com.libproxy.ucl.ac.uk/apps/doc/ RXHGVE173773054/TTDA?u=ucl_ttda&sid=bookmark-TTDA&xid =fe1522d7. Accessed 25 April 2024.

[314] Ryan Raffaelli, 'Reinventing Retail: The Novel Resurgence of Independent Bookstores', Harvard Business School Working Paper, No. 20-068, January 2020, p. 13.

Figure 8 Picture of the reinstated Dillon plaque, taken on 1 May 2024

Booksellers of the past contributed significantly to the cultural and intellectual lives of the people they served: they should not be hidden in the bookshelves of history. They are often, as this Element has hopefully shown, dynamic agents within the communications circuit. The women booksellers, moreover, as this Element proves, should more correctly be known as *formidable*, using the French term and meaning, rather than formidable in the English sense. True, they did use clothing and accessories to create and support their business personas – but there is not a ravelled cardigan in sight, in any description of the women here. Rather the evidence shows women who were successful at building up their own businesses, and running them during exceptional times. They worked at local, national, and international levels, influenced and defended book trade policy (and often helped create it); they trained, inspired, and made the Booksellers Association more accessible to junior booksellers; they helped support the transmission of ideas, from the radical to the most imaginative, to a new breed of reader. They were, in short, influential leading members of the book trade of the mid twentieth century.

It is entirely fitting, therefore, that as I wrote the final parts of this, news came in from Waterstones Gower Street that following another refurbishment, the plaque to Una Dillon has been spruced up, and now takes pride of place on the wall for everyone to see as they move upstairs from the ground floor[315] (see Figure 8). This literal uncovering and restoration sits alongside this Element to ensure these women are now visibly part of book trade history.

[315] Via email from Zoe Donaldson, Manager of Events at Waterstones Gower St, 1 May 2024.

Archival Sources

British Library, Book Trade Lives Sound Archive: Tapes C872/01/01. F 5891; C872/37. F7957. Tape 2, sides A and B; C872/37. F8119. Tape 10, side B; C872/83. F13596. Tape 16, sides A and B; C872/ 83. F13597. Tape 17, side A; C872/ 83. F13599. Tape 19, side A; C872/ 83. F13601. Tape 21, side B; C872/ 117. F17839. Tape 6, side A; C872/44. F8563. Tape 13, side B; C872/44. F8564. Tape 14, side A. (NB: visit was made in 2019, when some tapes could not be located, or had been sealed, by the BL. Currently all BL sound recordings are unavailable because of the cyber-attack which happened in October 2023.)

   Senate House Library Special Collections, Files MS926/8/1; MS926/8/2; MS926/2/4 /13

   LSE Special Collections, Files PIERCY/13/42; PIERCY/13/43

   BFI Special Collections, Carmen Dillon Collection Files LOC 157: ITM 16624, 16631, 16634, 16637, 16639, 16643, 16644, 16647

   National Archives: Files KV 2/1373, KV 2/1374, KV 2/1375 (Eva Collet Reckitt); KV 2/ 3364, KV 2/3365, KV 2/3366 (Margaret Mynatt)

   British Newspaper Archive: *The Bookseller*

Bibliography

Note: to save space, references to *The Bookseller* have been confined here to the major articles used. All other references can be found in the footnotes.

Adam, Ruth. *A Woman's Place*. Reissue: London: Persephone Books, 2000.

Adamson, Lesley. 'Red Eva Moves in on Foyles'. *The Guardian*, 23 August 1976, p. 9.

Anon. Collet's 25th Anniversary Lunch. *The Publishers Circular and Booksellers Record*, 25 April 1959, p. 281.

Anon. 'Farewell Luncheon for Miss Dillon'. *The Bookseller*, 16 September 1967, p. 1698.

Anon. 'Profile: Miss Elizabeth Weiler'. *Bookselling News*, May 1970, p. 40.

Anon. 'Thomas Joy; Doyen of the Book Trade Who Ran the Library at Harrods before Becoming the Head of Hatchards in Piccadilly'. *Daily Telegraph*, 23 April 2003.

Babbidge, Irene. *Beginning in Bookselling*. London: Andre Deutsch, 1965.

Babbidge, Irene. 'Revision without Tears: "On a February Morning"'. *The Bookseller*, 2 June 1956, pp. 1502–3.

Babbidge, Irene. 'Some Obstacles in the Way'. *The Bookseller*, 20 June 1964, pp. 2222–4.

Barker, Dennis. 'Obituary: Christina Foyle: The Power behind the Biggest Bookshop in the World, as Well as a Legendary Series of Literary Lunches'. *The Guardian*, 10 June 1999, p. 22.

Barker, R. E., and G. R. Davies (eds.). *Books Are Different: An Account of the Defence of the Net Book Agreement before the Restrictive Practices Court in 1962*. London: Macmillan, 1966.

Barnes, Earl. 'A New Profession for Women'. *The Atlantic Monthly* (1857–1932) Vol. 116, 1915: pp. 225–34.

Barr, Harry. 'What Una Dillon Didn't Tell the Princess . . .' *Publishing News*, 3 October 1986, p. 7.

Bohme, Harold. 'A Bookstore on the Campus'. In Eleanor Harman, ed. *The University as Publisher*. 1961, Toronto: Toronto University Press, pp. 157–61.

Booksellers Association. *Bookshops in the Cultural Life of the Nation*. n.d. www.booksellers.org.uk/BookSellers/BizFormFiles/da65dd35-ab98-44b6-b433-2ef12bafb293.pdf, Accessed 10 July 2019.

Bradley, Sue. (ed.). *The British Book Trade: An Oral History*. London: British Library, 2008.

Bredon, Kenneth. 'Margot Tyrie'. *The Bookseller*, 9 June 1984, pp. 2320–1.

Brimley Bowes, Major G. 'Education and the Book Trade'. *The Bookseller and Stationery Trades Journal*, August 1920, pp. 528–30.

Cadman, Eileen, Gail Chester, and Agnes Pivot. 'Getting the Ideas out: The Problems of Distribution'. In *Rolling Our Own: Women as Printers, Publishers, and Distributors*. London: Minority Press Group, 1981. pp. 88–98.

Caine, Danny. *How to Protect Bookstores and Why: The Present and Future of Bookselling*. Portland, OR: Microcosm, 2023.

Chambers, Matthew. *London and the Modernist Bookshop*. Cambridge: Cambridge University Press, 2020.

'Channels of Book Buying'. Books and the Public. [File Report]. Section XVII, p. 41. At: Place: University of Sussex. Available through: Adam Matthew, Marlborough, Mass Observation Online, www.massobserva tion.amdigital.co.uk.libproxy.ucl.ac.uk/Documents/Details/FileReport-1332. Accessed 3 August 2023].

Cholmeley, Jane. *A Bookshop of One's Own: How a Group of Women Set out to Change the World*. London: Mudlark, 2024.

Cocaign, Elen. 'The Left's Bibliophilia in Interwar Britain: Assessing Booksellers' Role in the Battle of Ideas'. *Twentieth Century Communism*, Vol. 4, Annual 2012, pp. 218–30.

Cole, Margaret. 'Books for the Multitude I: Reading without Buying'. *The Listener*, 22 December 1937, pp. 1388–9; 'Books for the Multitude II'. *The Listener*, 29 December 1937, pp. 1436–7; 'Books for the Multitude III'. *The Listener*, 5 January 1938, pp. 42–3; 'Books for the Multitude IV'. *The Listener*, 12 January 1938, pp. 95–6.

Cole, Margaret. *Books and the People*. London: Hogarth Press, 1938.

Cole, Margaret. 'Books for the People'. *The Times Literary Supplement*, 26 November 1938, p. 751.

Collingwood, Frances. 'Thus Speaks the Modern Bookseller'. *Books: Journal of the National Book League*, 1963, pp. 187–90.

Cook, Josh. *The Art of Libromancy: Selling Books and Reading Books in the Twenty-First Century*. Windsor: Biblioasis, 2023.

Cope, Dave. *Central Books: A Brief History 1939 to 1999*. London: Central Books, 1999.

Corp, William G. *Fifty Years: A Brief Account of the Associated Booksellers of Great Britain and Ireland 1895–1945*. Oxford: Basil Blackwell, 1948.

Crail, Mark. 'Fifty Years of Collets'. *Tribune*, 29 March 1984, p. 2.

Cunningham, John. 'Denials of the Misses Dillon'. *The Guardian*, 16 July 1986, p. 10.

Dark, Sidney. *The New Reading Public: A Lecture Delivered under the Auspices of the Society of Bookmen*. London: Allen & Unwin, 1922.

Darnton, Robert. *The Kiss of Lamourette: Reflections in Cultural History*. New York: Norton, 1990.

Daunt, James. Quoted in Ed Smith 'A Man with Plenty of Shelf Esteem'. *The Times*, 31 May 2011, p. 6.

Daunt, James. Quoted in James Dean, 'You Don't Have to Do Everything by the Book to Rescue Barnes & Noble'. *The Times*, 9 November 2019, p. 55.

Davies, Jessica. 'The Chaos Christina Left behind'. *Times*, 31 July 2001, pp. 4–5.

Delap, Lucy. 'Feminist Bookshop, Reading Cultures and the Women's Liberation Movement in Great Britain, c.1974–2000'. *History Workshop*, Vol. 81, No.1, 2016, pp. 171–96.

Deutsch, Jeff. *In Praise of Good Bookstores*. Princeton: Princeton University Press, 2022.

Dillon, Una. 'Floor Coverings for Bookshops'. In *Bookshop Equipment and Design*. London: Hutchinson, 1968. pp. 16–22.

Dillon, Una. 'Looking back and forward'. *The Bookseller*, 16 September 1967, pp. 1714–16.

Dillon, Una. 'The New Look in University Bookselling'. *Journal of Documentation*, Vol. 20, No. 4, 1964, pp. 198–202.

'Double U Tee Enn'. 'Women and Salesmanship'. *The Publishers' Circular and Booksellers' Record*, 11 June 1927, p. 725.

Dove, Richard. 'British Policy and the Refugees 1933–41'. *Journal of European Studies*, Vol. 29, No. 3, 1999, p. 321.

Edmonds, Elizabeth. 'Miss Light of the A.B.G.B.I.'. *The Bookseller*, 17 October 1946, p. 668.

Fallon, Judy. 'Books? I've Always Loved Them'. *The Sketch*, 23 May 1956, p. 340.

Foyle, Christina. 'The Bookseller and the Reading Public'. *Journal of the Royal Society of Arts*, Vol. 101, 18 September 1953, p. 779.

Frost, Simon. *Reading, Wanting, and Broken Economics*. New York: SUNY Press, 2021.

Fussell, Paul. *The Great War and Modern Memory*. Oxford: Oxford University Press, 1975.

Graves, Charles. 'More Celebrities in Cameo No 47: Christina Foyle'. *The Bystander*, Vol. 136, 24 November 1937, p. 281.

Grossman, Austin. 'Monocles Were Never Cool'. *The Atlantic*, 13 October 2019. www.theatlantic.com/technology/archive/2019/10/how-monocle-became-joke/599914/ Accessed 1 April 2022.

Guest, Katy. '*The Bookseller's Tale* by Martin Latham Review – a Literary Celebration'. *The Guardian*, 19 December 2020, www.theguardian.com/books/2020/dec/19/the-booksellers-tale-by-martin-latham-review-a-literary-celebration. Accessed 15 February 2024.

Hampden, John (ed.). *The Book World: A New Survey*. London: Thomas Nelson & Sons, 1935.

Hampden, John (ed.). *The Book World Today*. London: George Allen & Unwin Ltd, 1951.

Heginbothom, Margot. 'The Bookshop and the Community'. *The Bookseller*, 8 July1943, pp. 18–21.

Heginbothom, Margot. 'The Small Bookseller after the War'. *The Bookseller*, 16 September 1943, pp. 287–91.

Heginbothom, Margot. 'Orders in Uniform'. *The Bookseller*, 9 March, 1944, pp. 282–3.

Hentea, Marius. 'Monocles on Modernity'. *Modernism/Modernity*, Vol. 20, No. 2, 2013, p. 214.

Hodge, Warren. 'Christina Foyle, 88, the Queen of the London Bookstore, Dies'. *New York Times*, 11 June 1999, p. A31.

Horder, Mervyn. 'Gerti'. *The Bookseller*, 14 November 1986, p. 1954.

Ibbetson, Peter. 'On the Reluctance to Buy Books'. *The Nation and Athenaeum*, 5 March 1927, p. 753.

Ince, Robin. *Bibliomaniac: An Obsessive's Tour of the Bookshops of Britain*. London: Atlantic, 2022.

Joy, Thomas. *Mostly Joy: A Bookman's Story*. London: Michael Joseph, 1971.

Joy, Thomas. *The Bookselling Business*. London: Pitman, 1974.

Joy, Thomas. *The Truth about Bookselling*. London: Sir Isaac Pitman & Sons, 1964.

Keynes, John M. 'Are Books Too Dear?' *The Nation and Athenaeum*, 12 March 1927, p. 788.

Kvergic, Gerti. 'Book-Famished Europe'. *The Spectator*, 26 May 1944, pp. 472–3.

Kvergic, Gerti. 'How to Prevent the Sale of Books'. *The Bookseller*, 9 September 1967, p. 1648.

Kvergic, Gerti. 'Thoughts on the Psychology of Bookselling. *Bookselling News*, May/June 1971, pp. 14–5.

Lane, Allen. 'All about the Penguin Books'. *The Bookseller*, 22 May 1935, p. 497.

Langdon-Davies, Bernard N. *The Practice of Bookselling*. London: Phoenix House Ltd, 1951.

Latham, Martin. *The Bookseller's Tale*. London: Particular Books, 2020.

Laties, Andrew. *Rebel Bookseller*. New York: Seven Stories, 2011.

Leavis, Queenie D. *Fiction and the Reading Public*. London: Pimlico, 2000. The book was first published by Chatto & Windus in 1932.

Lyons, Rebecca. 'Thanks for Penguin: Women, Invisible Labour, and Publishing in the Mid-Twentieth Century'. In Juliana Dresvina, ed. *Thanks for Typing*: *Remembering Forgotten Women in History*. London: Bloomsbury, 2021. pp. 50–60.

McAleer, Joseph. *Popular Reading and Publishing in Britain 1914–1950*. Oxford: Clarendon Press, 1992.

Miller, Laura J. *Reluctant Capitalists*: *Bookselling and the Culture of Consumption*. Chicago: University of Chicago Press, 2006.

Morrison, Kathryn. 'Woolworth: Adding Character to the British High Street, 1909–1939'. *History of Retailing and Consumption*, Vol. 2, No.2, 2016, pp. 85–96.

Mountain, Penny. *Foyles*: *A Celebration*. London: Foyles, 2003.

Mumby, Frank. *Publishing and Bookselling*. London: Jonathan Cape, 1930.

Mumby, Frank. *Publishing and Bookselling*. New and Revised Ed. London: Jonathan Cape, 1949.

Mumby, Frank. *Publishing and Bookselling*. 3rd Ed. London: Jonathan Cape, 1954.

Mumby, Frank. *The Romance of Bookselling: A History from the Earliest Times to the Twentieth Century*. London: Chapman & Hall, 1910.

Mumby, Frank, with additions from Max Kenyon. *Publishing and Bookselling*. Revised & Enlarged Ed. London: Jonathan Cape, 1956.

Mumby, Frank A., and Ian Norrie. *Publishing and Bookselling*. 5th Ed. London: Jonathan Cape, 1974.

Neal, Lawrence E. *Retailing and the Public*. London: Allen & Unwin, 1932.

The Newbolt Report. 1921, p. 330. www.educationengland.org.uk/documents/newbolt/newbolt1921.html. Accessed 19 January 2022.

Newman, Fred. 'Dillons Special Report: 50th Anniversary Special'. *Publishing News*, 10 October 1986, pp. 6–11.

Norrie, Ian. *Mumby's Publishing and Bookselling in the Twentieth Century*. 6th Ed. London: Bell & Hyman, 1982.

Norrie, Ian. 'Obituary: Christina Foyle'. *The Independent*, 11 June 1999, p. 6.

Norrie, Ian. 'The Iron Lady of the Book Trade'. *The Bookseller*, 18 July 1999, p. 12.

Norrie, I., and Ink, G. 'The Literature of the Book: Retail Bookselling'. *Logos*, Vol. 15, No. 3, 2004. pp. 164–166. https://doi-org.libproxy.ucl.ac.uk/10.2959/logo.2004.15.3.164.

Norrie, Ian. 'Thomas Joy'. *The Independent*, 2 May 2003, p. 22.

Osborne, Huw. (ed.), *The Rise of the Modernist Bookshop: Books and the Commerce of Culture in the Twentieth Century*. Farnham: Ashgate, 2015.

Patterson, James, and Matt Eversmann. *The Secret Lives of Booksellers and Librarians*. London: Century, 2024.

Pocock, A. T. G. 'How the Bookseller Can Help the Publisher Sell More Books'. *The Bookseller*, 6 June 1959, pp. 1942–46.

Pollard, Marjorie. (Ed.). *Hilda M. Light: Her Life and Times*. London: All Women's Hockey Association, 1972.

Manwaring, Tom. 'All Set for Romance', *Sunday Telegraph*, 7 March 1965, p. 21.

Prime, John. 'Olive Parsons, Director of Collets Bookshops'. *The Bookseller*, 17 May 1996, p. 12.

Pullman, Philip. 'Bookselling in the UK'. 1 August 2017. www.philip-pullman.com/newsitem?newsItemID=26 Accessed 10 July 2019.

Raffaelli, Ryan. 'Reinventing Retail: The Novel Resurgence of Independent Bookstores'. Harvard Business School Working Paper No. 20-068 January 2020.

Raven, Susan. 'A Day in the Life of Christina Foyle'. *The Bookseller*, 22 May 1982, p. 1957.

Reckitt, Eva Collet. 'Twenty-Five Years in Charing Cross Road'. *The Bookseller*, 21 March 1959, pp. 1254–6.

R. E. S. 'Eva Reckitt'. *History Workshop*, Autumn 1976, No. 2, pp. 238–9.

Roy, Fernande. *Histoire de la librairie au Québec*. Québec: Leméac, 2000.

Rylance, Rick. *Literature and the Public Good*. Oxford: Oxford University Press, 2016.

Sadleir, Michael. 'Servants of Books: Their Privileges and Duties'. *The Bookseller and the Stationery Trades Journal* (October 1924), p. 80, and *The Publishers' Circular and Booksellers' Record* (4 October 1924), p. 469.

Samuel, Bill. *An Accidental Bookseller: A Personal Memoir of Foyles*. Oxford: Puxley Productions, 2019.

Sanders, Frank D. 'Miss H. M. Light'. *The Bookseller*, 8 November 1969, pp. 2486–7.

Sorel, Patricia. *Petite histoire de la librairie française*. Paris: La Fabrique, 2021.

Stevenson, Iain. 'Distribution and Bookselling'. In Andrew Nash, Claire Squires, and Ian R. Willison, eds. *The Cambridge History of the Book in Britain, Volume VII*. Cambridge: Cambridge University Press, 2019, pp.191–230.

Stockham, Peter. 'Obituary: Una Dillon'. *The Independent*, 17 April, 1993, p. 15.

Stockham, Peter. 'The Empire Born in an £800 shop'. *The Daily Mail*, 23 April 1993, p. 31.

Thacker, Andrew. '"A True Magic Chamber": The Public Face of the Modernist Bookshop'. *Modernist Cultures*, Vol. 11, No. 3, 2016, pp. 429–51.

Thacker, Andrew. 'Circulating Literature: Libraries, Bookshops and Book Clubs'. In Benjamin Kohlmann and Matthew Taunton, eds. *A History of 1930s British Literature*. Cambridge: Cambridge University Press, 2019. pp. 89–104.

Thomas, Niels Peter. 'Bookselling'. In Angus Phillips and Michael Bhaskar, eds. *The Oxford Handbook of Publishing*. Oxford: Oxford University Press, 2019, pp. 399–410.

Unwin, Philip. 'The New Reading Public'. *The Bookseller*, 5 April 1934, p. 184.

Unwin, Stanley. 'Concerning Sixpennies'. *The Times Literary Supplement*, 19 November 1938, p. 737.

Wainwright, Martin. 'Shelling out for Foyles Pets'. *The Guardian*, 8 December 1999, p. 2.

Waterstone, Tim. *The Face Pressed up against the Window*. London: Atlantic Books, 2019.

West, Elizabeth. *The Women Who Invented Twentieth-Century Children's Literature*. London: Routledge, 2023.

Wilson, N. 'Boots Book-lovers' Library and the Novel: The Impact of a Circulating Library Market on Twentieth Century Fiction'. *Information and Culture*, Vol. 49, No. 4, 2014, pp. 427–49.

Woolf, Virginia. *A Room of One's Own*. Originally published in London by the Hogarth Press in 1929. Edition used here: London, Penguin Modern Classics, 2000.

Woolf, Virginia. *The Common Reader, Vol. I*. Ed. Andrew MacNeillie. London: Vintage, 2003. (First published by The Hogarth Press in 1925).

Young, Charles. 'Books and the Public: The Bookseller's Point of View'. *The Nation and Athenaeum*. 16 April 1927, pp. 43–4.

Acknowledgements

This Element is dedicated to all the women booksellers out there, past and present, with an apology that this Element only scratches the surface of the histories to be told, and a promise that this is just a starting point for more. I have been extremely lucky to have been supported in this research by many people who have shared stories, possible links, and materials with me: so thanks go to Professor Jo Stockham, who has so generously helped with Una Dillon's history via papers from her father, Peter Stockham, who was Una's successor as manager of the bookshop; to Teresa Grimes, working on a history of Una's Oscar-award winning sister, Carmen, for sharing news about the wonderful material in Carmen's archive held at the BFI; to all the special collections staff who helped me at the BFI, Senate House Special Collections, and the LSE Special Collections, and to the staff at the Cambridge University Library who brought me trolleys and trolleys of *The Bookseller* to look through. Special thanks to Rachel Calder and all those involved in making *The Bookseller* digitised, which has made an enormous difference to the speed of research in this area, too, and to Zoe Donaldson and the staff at Waterstones Gower St, who I have hounded over the past few years about the missing Dillon plaque, and who have been so helpful in making sure this is now back, in pride of place, in the shop.

To Meryl Halls, Kate Gunning, Emma Bradshaw, and Sheila O'Reilly at the Booksellers Association – thank you to you all for being so inspirational as successors to the women included here in terms of Association work; it's brilliant to see another woman bookseller, Fleur Sinclair, elected as President this year, following on from Hazel Broadfoot. To Mark Thornton from Bookshop.org, for so many talks, plans, and enthusiasms around bookshops, and to all the staff at my local bookshop, Toppings in Ely, for helping with many bookshop-related book orders over the past years (I can't promise this is going to stop!) To my colleague Daniel Boswell, for helping create and protect some spaces for research time in a challenging few years, and to Eben Muse for sharing the love for bookshop-related work for so many years.

Finally, to my family, who arguably know more about Una Dillon now than they ever wanted to, to all my friends who came to my Inaugural Lecture in 2022, and helped me believe this was research people would be interested in, and to Rachel, Angie, and my swimming group of utterly amazing women who have done more than they will ever know to help me get this finished.

Permissions

Permission given by Professor Jo Stockham to use images (Figures 1, 3, 4, 5, and 7) from her father's collection.

Permission given by the family of Douglas Logan, via Senate House Library Special Collections, to quote from his papers held there.

Permission given by Zoe Donaldson to use the image of the reinstated Una Dillon plaque (Figure 8).

Cambridge Elements ☰

Publishing and Book Culture

SERIES EDITOR
Samantha J. Rayner
University College London

Samantha J. Rayner is Professor of Publishing and Book
Cultures at UCL. She is also Director of UCL's Centre for
Publishing, co-Director of the Bloomsbury CHAPTER
(Communication History, Authorship, Publishing, Textual
Editing and Reading) and co-Chair of the Bookselling
Research Network.

ASSOCIATE EDITOR
Leah Tether
University of Bristol

Leah Tether is Professor of Medieval Literature and
Publishing at the University of Bristol. With an academic
background in medieval French and English literature and
a professional background in trade publishing, Leah has
combined her expertise and developed an international
research profile in book and publishing history from
manuscript to digital.

About the Series

This series aims to fill the demand for easily accessible, quality texts available for teaching and research in the diverse and dynamic fields of Publishing and Book Culture. Rigorously researched and peer-reviewed Elements will be published under themes, or 'Gatherings'. These Elements should be the first check point for researchers or students working on that area of publishing and book trade history and practice: we hope that, situated so logically at Cambridge University Press, where academic publishing in the UK began, it will develop to create an unrivalled space where these histories and practices can be investigated and preserved.

Cambridge Elements ⬛

Publishing and Book Culture

Bookshops and Bookselling

Gathering Editor: Eben Muse

Eben Muse is Senior Lecturer in Digital Media at Bangor
University and co-Director of the Stephen Colclough Centre
for the History and Culture of the Book. He studies the impact
of digital technologies on the cultural and commercial space of
bookselling, and he is part-owner of a used bookstore in the
United States.

ELEMENTS IN THE GATHERING

Printed in the United States
by Baker & Taylor Publisher Services